PRAISE FOR MICHAEL HARDING

'Harding is a self-deprecating and winsome writer whose bittersweet musings on middle-age, loneliness and the search for spiritual enlightenment … are leavened by an incredibly dry and unforced wit' *Metro Herald*

'Often funny, occasionally disturbing and not without its moments of deep sadness, Harding has peeled back his soul and held it out on the palm of his hand for all to see' Christine Dwyer-Hickey

'A repository of modern man's deepest fears, Harding emerges as something of an embattled hero for our times … It's rare for a memoir to demand such intense emotional involvement, and rarer still for it to be so fully rewarded' *Sunday Times*

'Hilarious, and tender, and mad, and harrowing, and wistful, and always beautifully written. A wonderful book' Kevin Barry

'I read this book in one sitting … Beautifully written … *Staring at Lakes* gives us permission to be lost, sick, sad, creative, happy and compassionate – in short, to be human' Mary McEvoy, *Irish Independent*

'This memoir grabs you from the outset and holds

Michael Harding is an author and playwright. His creative chronicle of ordinary life in the Irish midlands is published as a weekly column in *The Irish Times*. He has written numerous plays for the Abbey Theatre, including *Una Pooka*, *Misogynist* and *Sour Grapes*, and has published three novels, *Priest*, *The Trouble with Sarah Gullion* and *Bird in the Snow* as well as a bestselling memoir, *Staring at Lakes*.

MICHAEL HARDING

Hanging with the Elephant

HACHETTE
BOOKS
IRELAND

First published in 2014 by Hachette Books Ireland
First published in paperback in 2015.

1

A CIP catalogue record for this title is available from the British Library.

ISBN: 9781444783148

Typeset in AGaramond and MrsEaves by Bookends Publishing Services, Dublin
Printed by CPI Group (UK) Ltd, Croydon, CR0 4YY

Hachette Books Ireland policy is to use papers that are natural, renewable
and recyclable products and made from wood grown in sustainable forests.
The logging and manufacturing processes are expected to conform to the
environmental regulations of the country of origin.

Hachette Books Ireland
8 Castlecourt Centre, Castleknock, Dublin 15, Ireland

A division of Hachette UK Ltd
Carmelite House, 50 Victoria Embankment, London EC4Y 0DZ

www.hachette.ie

For Brendan

I GOT ITCHY feet one time and left the beloved. I headed for Paris, but ended up in Mullingar. It was all because I knew too much – or thought I did. I knew who I was and I knew where I was going, in terms of my life journey, and I had decided it was time to leave Leitrim. Simple as that. *It is important to see the world*, I told myself. Going to seed in rural Ireland was not an option. So I presumed I was finished with the little cottage in the hills above Lough Allen, the home my beloved and I had set up thirteen years earlier. But of course I was wrong.

Five years later I returned. Knocking on the door, I said, 'I'm sorry I ran away. Will you please let me in?'

'But why,' she asked, 'did you go away?'

I don't know,' I confessed. 'OK, so maybe I was worried that I hadn't seen enough of the world and thought I might begin another life in Paris or elsewhere, despite the fact that I was over fifty.'

'Yes,' she said. 'And where did that get you?'

'To Mullingar,' I confessed.

'So you didn't get very far at all, did you?'

'No.'

After five years in Mullingar, I was on the flat of my back with a gigantic prostate, colitis, mental burnout and tears filling my eyes. 'Hold me,' I begged her. 'I'm a ruined man.'

And she did. And every day I sat up in bed, sipping a little soup and writing a few pages on the computer until I had a book finished, which was published and did very well and won a few national prizes, and then suddenly I was out of the bed again, going around the country, talking to audiences about how little I knew about anything. It's amazing how consoling the general public finds it to meet someone who knows nothing.

And I suppose what I now accept is that I most definitely know nothing. If I had used that insight as my guide on the road of life, like a route on the sat-nav, I wouldn't have gone down so many cul-de-sacs. Knowing things can be a big problem. It can lead a man astray. It's a delusion to think you know it all. In fact, it may be a delusion to think you know anything. Although it's not easy to sustain a life based on knowing nothing. Or to admit you know nothing, especially when, like me, you're trying to write another book.

I went to a psychotherapist about all this. She told me I needed meaning in my life.

'But I've tried Christianity,' I said. 'And I've tried Buddhism. Neither of them seems to work for me.'

'And why did you leave your wife?'

'I found marriage a bit boring,' I replied. 'And besides, she had a different view of how to fill a dishwasher.'

'And why did you go back?'

'Because I was wrong – about the dishwasher. And now I think maybe marriage does work.'

She didn't say anything else. I suppose that's because she's a psychotherapist.

And what I find most difficult of all is that being a man is wildly more complicated than it was in my father's time. Nowadays, it's essential to be liked. And men want to be understood. They want to be held. They want to go to therapists and they want to cry on television. Men are expected to be tender and human and loving, and to know when to hold their partner and when not to.

I'm told that in the olden days, men spent their time in the fields making hay and had no feelings, and women were inside stirring pots of stew that later everyone ate, at the bare board table on the flagstone floor, in a kind of monastic silence, as they all inhabited the bliss of being a family.

That must have been really peaceful. Everything was simple. A man knew where he stood. In daylight, he wasn't unlike a horse, a thing that lived outside, only coming indoors late in the evening. He grunted over his soup, dozed by the fire or smoked a pipe as his children grew up around him, and sometimes in the night he surprised his wife in silent love-making with the tenderness of a child.

When I returned home, I was sixty and I hoped I might just have enough wit to be a competent lover by then; because more than anything else in the world, a man dreams of being in love.

I certainly wouldn't like to imply that I'm a great romantic, but there was one phrase I kept coming back to when I was recovering from depression.

'Hold me.'

That's all I could say to my beloved. It was sad and pathetic, and I was embarrassed, but I said it over and over again, and she did it over and over again. She held me.

If I were a romantic, I might have used other phrases. I might have used the kind of phrases James Bond uses, and I'd throw them at her because she's a beautiful person. I'd scatter them before her feet. But I didn't. Not when I was recovering. I was speechless most of the time when we were alone and, I discovered, a man is not very attractive in striped pyjamas.

In public or on stage, it's different. I'm fine. I have no bother talking to three hundred people, and sharing my feelings. But when I'm in a room on a one-to-one basis, I get lost. Dumbfounded. I can never find the right word. Except for that phrase – hold me.

And then of course there was the case of my poor mother, who lived so long and who for so many years had nobody to hold her at all.

6   THAT'S WHAT I was thinking on a bright May morning in 2014, two years after my mother had died. On that particular morning, my beloved was returning from Poland where she had been for six weeks. I woke early. The room was still dark but through the window I could see the sun's rays edging over the mountain. The sky was clear. The rain clouds had not yet gathered in from the ocean to cover Leitrim with that oppressive grey which makes humans in this part of the world feel so desolate and melancholic.

A glass of water sat beside my iPhone on the headboard above my head. The curtain was half open and my clothes were on the floor. I reached up to turn the phone on and listen to the morning news on BBC Radio 4. Then I got out of bed, using the phone as a lamp, and went to the bathroom. I had slept soundly through the night, and I relieved myself in a single and marvellous flow from my bladder and felt an enormous sense of well-being.

The reason for this sense of well-being was because in my early fifties, I'd been going to the bathroom every forty minutes, resulting from an enlarged prostate, and I was constantly walking around with the unpleasant sensation that my bladder was never empty. Then at sixty, after a successful operation to reduce the size of my prostate, I became a new man. I became like one of those Cavan men I have always admired; the ones who can down six pints without leaving the high stool and then go outside under the arch and piss with the ferocity of an officer's horse.

I shaved, observing myself in the mirror, lathering my face, neck and cheeks with a green slimy gel and then pulled the razor blade closely down each side, line by line, like a window cleaner, ensuring not to touch the small goatee that gave my chin some respectability. For years, I'd never bothered shaving. So I wasn't good at it. And I only started wearing a goatee when I began visiting the therapist. I thought I might look more awake, or at least less mad, and more inclined to take the world seriously with a sharp little bush on my chin.

The therapist raised her eyebrow.

'And of course there's always something erotic about shaving,' I said, because I always tried to dredge up something for the therapist.

She raised the other eyebrow so I didn't pursue the topic. I was wearing some round-rimmed glasses I had bought in a chemist earlier that day for €5. I thought they might enhance the goatee. I wanted to look like a psychiatrist; it was a kind of defence mechanism, I suppose.

The sun had not yet risen fully over the ridge of the mountain, but the faint grey light in the sky was intensifying above Sliabh an Iarainn, and the trees in the garden were almost visible. I put on fresh underwear, clean socks and a tight-fitting shirt, with brown cord trousers, and had a look at myself in the mirror.

The smell of chicken and onion wafted from a pot on the cooker in the kitchen.

That will make the place feel homely when she arrives, I'd thought.

I'd bought the chicken in Scollan's of Drumshanbo, a bright Gala shop that combines a family supermarket with a butcher's counter and also provides hot dinners in a small restaurant at the front. For me and many others in Leitrim, it is a lifeline, a trading post, a kind of community centre. I'd brought the chicken home and put it in a pot with carrots, potatoes, onions, parsley and soup mix, and let it boil slowly on the cooker the previous evening.

In the bathroom, I splashed my neck with Boss because I needed to smell good too. Who knows how ravenous we might be for each other by the time we got through a bottle of wine. I know men aren't very reliable in matters of sexual performance when they pass the age of fifty, but it's amazing what a period of abstinence can achieve.

I sucked in my stomach, powdered the underwear and squirted more Boss on all sides.

That morning the beloved planned to fly from Modlin airport in Warsaw at 9 a.m. and arrive in Dublin before noon. We intended to meet at the airport. Then we would drive home and I would lift the lid off the pot and she would see the amazing soup, with carrots and onions and potatoes and parsley floating on top and a plump chicken sitting in the middle.

And yet, I was sorry that the six weeks had come to an end. My solitary retreat was closed. Our brief separation over. The soup was in the pot. The bird was well and truly cooked.

I had everything prepared. I was trussed up as well as a pot-bellied old man of sixty can manage to truss himself, because I still harboured intense fantasies of an erotic nature and dreamed of fulfilling them with the lady wife when she returned and had washed down the chicken with a bottle of Bordeaux. I get excited when I've been alone for a while, and then suddenly the day of her return arrives and I get an urge to hold her. Even though I usually just stand there at the airport like a gobdaw when she wheels her trolley through the arrivals gate after some of her travels. I say things like, 'Well, how did you get on?' as if she had only been away for twenty minutes looking for a particular book in the library. I want to hug and hold her but sometimes I don't because it seems too emotional a risk in public. I am embarrassed to lash out all that girly feeling at an airport in front of so many men in visor jackets and peaked caps.

'What exactly do you think is girly about being emotional?' my therapist wondered one day. I couldn't answer her. And when I thought again about airports, I had to admit that the arrival lounges are usually stuffed with men happily flinging their emotions in all directions. Men with sun-burned faces, short trousers, sandals and silly hats going way over the top emotionally, shouting their lovers' names, grabbing their wives by the buttocks and pushing their uncouth tongues into their lovers' faces like they were in an adult movie.

'So what's so girly about showing emotions?' the therapist repeated.

'Nothing,' I admitted. Although in my neck of the woods, people are masters of emotional restraint. The conventional salutation in Leitrim among neighbours is a minimal nod of the head, and there are no lovers,

10

just husbands who after being parted from their wives for a very long time might just risk whispering in her ear something like, 'So, there you are.'

I can cook, but I rarely bother. In fact, I am ashamed of all the meals I have failed to cook for the beloved over the years, because I was too busy playing the flute or watching television or working on another book or renouncing the world in one of those self-absorbing private meditation sessions that used to isolate me in my studio for hours and sometimes years. I know there are men who serve their lovers steak in lean slices, blood raw, with fresh salads drenched in exotic oils, and other men who have a reputation for tossing a few things around in a wok for three minutes and dazzling their lovers with the aphrodisiac spontaneity of their noodles. But I never got beyond doing a chicken in a pot of soup the way my mother used to do it. The chicken bent over, like a dead monk at prayer in a jungle swamp.

I think many men are glad when their wives or lovers go away for a while. It allows them time to play house on their own. To fantasise about what it would be like if they had remained unmarried. Being alone, they feel they have permission to surf the internet, check out porn sites and leave the bed unmade for weeks.

And it's a serious thing to leave a man alone at any time. There's no telling what he'll get up to. Men catch ideas like an open mouth attracts flies. They worry about things.

11

They rearrange the furniture. They make big decisions. They opt out of marriage. They plan affairs. They change jobs. They resign from the club. They drink beer, smoke dope and watch football. They use their wives' toiletries in the bath and never clean up. In fact, it was when I was alone for a weekend that I once tried to shave my pubic hair in a fit of erotic passion after downing a bottle of wine while watching a programme on Sky about what young men do nowadays to enhance their sex lives. I lathered shaving cream all over the target area and then with a Wilkinson Sword triple blade scraped it all off, leaving myself tender and bald. It felt supersensitive. It reminded me of being a baby. But I anticipated vast increases of sensual pleasure during future orgasms. Or at least that is what the guy in the television programme had claimed would happen.

And it wasn't easy explaining the results to the beloved when she arrived home from a friend's funeral – and to be honest it didn't even make any difference except that I got an ingrown hair, which created a boil of puss under the skin and I had to go to the doctor a few months later.

I remember one morning in the sauna gazing at a younger man whose chest was smooth but whose legs were as hairy as a gorilla and I suspected he may have shaved more than his chin. I was even tempted to enquire, there in the intimacy of the steam room, whether or not he had ever ventured between his legs with the razor and if so had he ever experienced any trouble with ingrown hairs, but discretion is the yardstick in the steam rooms of rural Ireland, so I decided to say nothing.

I am one of those men who likes to think he can survive without women, even though experience keeps telling me the opposite. I find a liberation in my own smell, the masculinity of a full sink, the nonchalance of dirty underwear piled on an armchair in the sitting room, and the kind of personal chaos that makes women doubt their own sanity for loving such savages and makes women wonder if they were utterly mad the day they walked up the aisle of some church long ago in a big white meringue of silk and satin to pledge loyalty to a half-evolved Neanderthal with a fragrant penis. A solitary man in a house is an unfolding horror movie, like fungus in an unwashed cupboard or the blue mould that grows in coffee cups that have been abandoned under chairs or on the cistern in the toilet or hidden on the window sill behind unopened curtains and forgotten about until the morning of her return.

Not that I was entirely delighted when my beloved told me she was going off to Poland, because I had become dependent on her. Even though she would only be gone for six weeks, I would now be forced to stand alone – something I had done rarely since June 2011 when I had suffered a physical and nervous breakdown. Apart from a few weekends here and there, or the fortnight she spent in London, I had rarely been so completely abandoned.

Every so often, men get the urge to create sheds and special no-go areas, like rooms to meditate in or rooms to work in, but all that insulation never solved anything for me. I have a little studio in the back garden but I might only be there for five minutes, with an image of the Buddha or a book about theatre or a low whistle in the key of D, when suddenly I would be overwhelmed by the terror of being alone and my desperate need for company even if it was just to have a cup of tea with her.

And then her presence would relieve me from all my morose introspection. I wouldn't have to worry about the meaning of life or the bleak prospect of death or any of the other great philosophical issues that prohibit me from washing dishes or making the bed, as long as I could worry about what she might want. When I told this to the therapist, she looked at me for a long time before saying that I wasn't unusual.

'Many men tend to orbit their loved ones like dysfunctional satellites,' she said. 'They obsess about the woman in order to avoid examining their own lives. The minutiae of the partner's life becomes their agenda. When does she want dinner? How does she like her tea? What she prefers to watch on the television. All those things become a narrative that absorbs men beyond the scope of their own nostalgia. It's the only reason why some men remain married. They find it soothing.'

And it occurred to me that perhaps this was precisely why the beloved needed to go to Poland. She needed a break. She needed to get away from me. I may have been driving her mad.

As a wise woman said to me one time: men spend the first half of their lives running away from women and the second half running after them. One way or another, I encouraged her to go, and I was glad when she bought her plane ticket. Because, beneath everything else, I had a real sense of purpose about being alone for a long period.

Not that long ago, depression had manifested in my life like my own private Dracula. I had spent months with him in the same room when I was ill and now, two years later, he rarely looked in the window. Although, I suspected that he was still lurking somewhere at the end of the garden, and I was always afraid that if I was alone for a long period of time, he might just knock on the door again. And that fear made me dependent on other people for company.

Although there is something in me that never stops craving solitude. So for six weeks in the spring of 2014, when she planned to be in Poland, I planned a journey to the interior. I was going on retreat. I would confront the unruly elephant of my own mind and I would use the ropes of meditation, discipline and single-pointed concentration to make that elephant sit still.

At least that's what the various gurus on YouTube were

suggesting. 'Depression is a lack of control,' they said. You become filled with disturbing emotions, with anxiety, fear or melancholy, and that drags you down. But if you can control the mind – the great elephant of consciousness – you can observe all those emotions coming and going, rising and falling; and you can watch them, hold them, and allow them to be. You can wait for them to evaporate like soft clouds evaporate into the sky or let them rinse your body like clouds turning into rain. One way or another you can bear them and quieten them, until eventually your mind can become as calm as an elephant at ease with itself, or as clear as a blue sky.

I wanted to stop going about the world like a blue-arsed fly, from one pile of dung to the next utterly consumed with anxiety and occasionally possessed by Dracula. I wanted to be still and chilled and full of compassion for the universe. I wanted to be a blue sky. I wanted to be a calm elephant. I wanted to be what the wise ones in robes on YouTube said I could be. Surely that wasn't too much to ask?

And if Dracula or any other personification of my anxieties knocked on the door, I would let them in and sit them down and gently accept them. I had read all the books on how to be compassionate with myself, and how to find a mindful path out of depression, and how to survive in the swamplands of the soul.

And when she came home, I would make a great splash. I would give her a great welcome. It would be like she was meeting a new man. And we would have a banquet. I would feed her one of Mister Scollan's finest chickens in a soup of fresh vegetables.

And I'll never know what I'd been through at all.

WE HAD BOTH ended up in a panic the morning she was heading off. I had booked the same hotel as we had stayed in on the night my memoir had received the Irish Book of the Year Award at the end of 2013. On that occasion, I had squeezed myself into a dress suit and clipped a dickie-bow round my neck with inflated pride, as if writing a book and winning an award were of some significance or that they might protect me from death. But when we returned to the same deluxe room of that Ballsbridge hotel four months later, it was being refurbished, and the painters' ladders lay in the corridor and the dizzy prize-winning ceremony seemed like it had all happened years earlier.

The award had been a transient moment. The book was nothing more than the tracks of an animal or footprints on a beach long since rearranged by the tide. The morning after the award ceremony, the blue glass trophy was sitting in the bath, for some reason I can't remember. We shared breakfast in bed, and then I did a radio interview and then we drove home.

But now I was lying on the bed with a terrible hangover, and the heating had been on all night, drying my tongue to the texture of sandpaper.

She was gone. She was on the plane. 'Thank Christ,' I said with relief, speaking to my own image in the mirror across from the bed. 'The panic is over.'

Those were the very words I used. I was still in the hotel an hour after she had rushed from the room. I was looking at the message she had texted from the boarding gate:

Just about got here in time.

We had decided to go to Dublin the day before the flight and stay over, rather than drive from Leitrim in the middle of the night. We'd had a Chinese meal in a very swanky restaurant near the hotel, early in the evening. The dumplings we had for starters were hand-made. They would have made a meal on their own. The soy sauce just sprinkled on the rice was fit for emperors.

I suppose the restaurant would have been full during the boom. I could imagine government ministers on their way home dropping in, or bankers with grey hair and gold cuff-links entertaining their mistresses, or journalists swapping jokes with the oily-skinned bosses of corporate Ireland. It had the air of a film set where great things had been enacted. Where historical events had been dreamed up. But the good times were over. The pile on the carpet was still thick and soft, and the lighting was just as delicate and the white tablecloths just as starched, but there was nobody there. They even had an early bird menu so that ordinary folks like us could afford to eat between five and eight, but even with a special offer of won ton soup, noodles and a choice of three main courses for €23, the place was empty. A famous journalist with grey hair and a cream linen suit sat at a table across from us reading a book. I kept trying to see the title, but I couldn't.

The beloved and me are used to each other, so we don't need to make much idle talk when we're in a restaurant. I look at her sometimes and I don't know what goes on in her head. The closer we get, and the longer we are together, the more mysterious she becomes. And the more transfixed we are by a shared silence. Of course she is used to my appetite for other people's conversations. I'm nosey. Not that I was eavesdropping on the journalist, though he did take up

20

his phone once when it buzzed, and I stopped chewing in order to listen, but it was only a text and he didn't reply. The beloved was lifting her full spoon from the won ton soup at that moment – when his phone buzzed – and she too stopped. Her soup spoon frozen in midair, because she knows me and my insatiable curiosity.

So that's where we were, eating our noodles with the masters of the universe, or at least one correspondent for a national newspaper, whom we recognised from his appearances on television. But the universe was empty apart from one further group of men at a table in the distance, whispering in London accents. And it was such a good meal that the bottle of wine we drank during the main course only kicked in three hours later at about midnight, when we were sitting in the lounge of the hotel with a nightcap. There too business was slow. An old country and western singer, a great bear of a man with dyed black hair, was trying to impress a thin woman in a grey dress with anecdotes about travelling around Ireland in a van years earlier when he had his own showband. She was recording it all, though when she went to the toilet her high heels clip-clopped with irritation on the parquet floor and her face looked as drained as an empty paper bag. We had Hennessy brandies and the wine kicked in so well that I suggested another bottle for the bedroom. After all, she was going away for six weeks. I would miss her. There would be no fun without her. And she was going to meet Polish friends, other artists, new people. She would be going to exhibitions and operas, and eating lots of Polish and Russian dumplings. So it was a big night for both of us. And since we had splashed out on a good hotel, and were safely situated in a deluxe room and there was a bus from just outside the hotel to the airport in the morning, we deserved another drink. That was my contention. And that's when the trouble started.

Up we went to the eighth floor. I was carrying two brandies, two wine glasses, one bottle of Bordeaux and the key of the room, all on a round tray. I'm always spilling things but we managed to get in, get the lights on and put down the drinks without losing anything.

Pussy Riot had been interviewed on an Irish chat show a few days earlier, which we watched on YouTube, and we couldn't take our eyes off the little laptop screen. We got so excited about how disastrous the interview turned out, that I suggested another bottle of wine. Which cost another €28.

'We have spent more money on drink than we did on the meal,' she observed.

'Ah, yes,' I replied, 'but it's a special occasion. We are separating.'

'It's only for a few weeks,' she said.

'True,' I replied. 'But that could be a long time with a mind as fragile as mine.'

She was leaving me. That was the fact.

'Beloved,' I said to her in the hotel room, as we came

to the end of the Bordeaux, 'I have rarely been alone these past three years. And now this is our last night together before your flight. So it is a very special occasion.'

She agreed, not certain what I had in mind. I had drink in mind. More drink. Lots of drink. An endless flow of drink.

So a youth from Latvia arrived with further wine. I gave him €30 and told him to keep the change, and on we went, drinking and watching various other YouTube videos. Pussy Riot. Panti Bliss. Johnny Rotten and Judge Judy. Tommy Tiernan. And live webcams in Warsaw to see if it was snowing. I drank most of the second bottle, laughing at the videos, until she brushed her teeth and got into bed and I assured her that I had set my alarm for 6.30 a.m.

She was asleep in minutes and already I felt alone. I was embracing the dark. I was beginning a great adventure into the interior of my own psyche. I would be still, silent and alone, eating like a monk, my eyes glued to the flickering candle as I meditated my way into the dark interior of the unconscious. I would find what was in there. *Who was in there.* What had made me unwell? In what way is depression just a door into a deeper sense of self? What are the possibilities of compassion both for ourselves and others that awaken when we allow all the pain inside us to surface?

There was no point in setting the bar too low. I might even find out what possessed me to shave my cock. I would

23

come to realise everything. Alone for forty-odd days, a cosy calm abiding, I would see beyond the self in which I was isolated, to the miracle of Being, in which we are all one and where there is no coming or going, and no death or birth.

My shelves were full of books on self-improvement, paths to enlightenment, loving kindness and how to escape depression. But the time for reading was over. The time for doing had arrived. The day was upon me and I would not be afraid. I would not cry out for anyone to hold me. Because sometimes a man must travel into the darkness – alone.

I closed the laptop, brushed my teeth in the bathroom, turned off the lights and slipped in beside her.

It seemed like I was asleep for five minutes when the sound of a trumpet on my iPhone indicated that another day was already waiting.

'Beloved,' I whispered, touching the nape of her neck on the pillow beside me. 'Beloved. 'Tis time to rise.'

But I had got the call-time arseways.

'You said 6.30 a.m,' I protested.

'Yes,' she said, 'I need to check in for 6.30.' And she sprang up so suddenly in the bed that I thought she might bounce off the ceiling.

'Fuck it,' I muttered to myself. I never saw anyone move so fast through their morning ablutions in my life. She showered, dressed, zipped her bags closed and was out the door in less than fifteen minutes. In that time, I had contacted Reception, a taxi had arrived and when we got down to the lobby along a corridor smelling of paint, I could see the taxi's roof sign through the glass door. She got in and I mouthed the words 'I love you' through the window before the taxi slipped out the gate and into the grey drizzle of a Dublin morning.

And I went back to bed. I dozed a bit until she texted from the boarding gate, and when she did, I phoned her back instantly and wished her a safe journey and apologised for getting so drunk and told her I'd miss her terribly. In the two years since my illness, I hadn't known what it was to live without her. I had been with her all the time. Day and night. And there was something final about the phone line going dead that morning. As if I might never hear her again. I stared at the screen.

'Well, that's it,' I said. 'She's gone. She's on the plane. May God help me now.'

God or Buddha or Simone Weil. Anyone would do. It didn't matter. I would lean on any god who helped me stand alone, because I believed it imperative that, as a couple, we should not be tied to each other. We should not be gazing at each other all the time but, together, gazing outwards into the universe. We should be like Sartre and de Beauvoir, I thought, and not the Tweedledum and Tweedledee of an Irish marriage.

'Would you like a cup of tea?' asks Tweedledum.

'I don't know,' Tweedledee replies. 'Would you?'

'Will we have our dinner now?' asks Tweedledum.

'Whatever you think,' Tweedledee replies.

'And what are you thinking, in your own little head?' Tweedledum might wonder eventually, but never ask for fear it would flummox Tweedledee entirely.

You see them sometimes in the supermarkets, tethered to the same trolley. He's in a daze. He might see corn flakes on the shelf. He likes his corn flakes. He reaches for the packet. She takes it from him and switches it for the muesli. And when his fingers touch the honey jar, she points to the organic one, and his fingers obey. 'That's better for you,' she says. And he doesn't disagree.

On the other hand, when he's puffed up at a dinner table and she knows he's going to start a conversation about bankers that will swiftly turn into a monologue to make everyone cringe, she just drops her head and listens graciously because she understands him. She is one with him. They are a single being. And as he gets into his stride, she rises from the table and says, 'I'm off to bed.' The wind goes out of his sails. He lasts another few minutes before following her. Because she is his 'other'. She is the listener. She is the monitor and mentor. It is pointless speaking when she is absent. It's even pointless living when she has left and gone for ever. And I have seen them too, the widows, bewildered in their slippers, struggling with the tax forms and the car insurance for a few years after he is

26

dead and then she too fades, glad to close her eyes for ever and be planted with him because there is no individuality or separateness left in her. And they become one again in the clay.

Maybe that's why I ended up in Mullingar. I was like a dog chasing its own tail. When I was with her, I wanted to be alone; when I was alone, I longed to be with her.

It's a common affliction of the male psyche, summed up by my mother when I threw my toys out of the pram. 'You're never satisfied,' she'd said.

'But you'll be fine on your own,' the beloved assured me in a text from the boarding gate. 'I really need to go.' And I suspected some lightness in her footfall as she walked the tarmac and up the stairway of the Ryanair flight and took her seat just inside the cabin door.

27

I FELL BACK asleep, my body still vibrating with the excess of alcohol in my system, though I slept soundly until after midday when I got a text from Eastern Europe.

Arrived at Modlin. Great flight. Cold but no rain.

I resisted phoning her. She wouldn't like that. She'd say it was wasting money. So I texted.

Great. You got there safely.

Yes. Friends at the airport to meet as planned.

That's great.

Long pause before next signal from her.

R U OK?

Yes I'm OK.

New text from me.

I mean I'm fine.

From her.

What will you do?

From me.

Go back to Leitrim this evening and be miserable.
Ha ha.

From her.

That's grand. Do that. Won't call you. Wastes money. You can get me on Facebook. Use text in emergency.

I watched the screen for a long while to see if she would say anything else. I couldn't think of a new text either. So I presumed we were finished.

Sitting up in the bed, I couldn't resist my image staring out at me from the mirror on the wall; him that was going to be my constant and perhaps only companion for the next few weeks.

29

'So why are you looking so miserable?' I asked. But the image in the mirror didn't reply. Apart from asking me the same question. I looked old, hung over and as sad as a wet field that even the cattle have abandoned.

I got up and stood sideways, just to get a better view. It was the same mirror in which I had examined myself, dressed in a tuxedo on the night of the book awards. It's not just that I was overweight, but my stomach had expanded out of proportion to the rest of my body. I felt like a whale but I looked like a duck. I walked naked, watching myself in all eight mirrors in the room and making critical comments.

I don't know why men begin to resemble ducks as they grow older. The rump expands at the rear and the belly expands forward. The spine begins to make an S shape in order to carry everything as the muscles collapse and the bloated gut flags and falls towards earth. It's a shape that has been bred into men over generations of affluence. It should make me ashamed, when I see what I've done to my body over a lifetime, considering that most human beings are merely skin and bone and barely get enough food to sustain themselves. But men don't feel shame too often. That's bred out of us as well. Sometimes I see friends crossing the floor of a hotel foyer like turkey cocks, proud of every ounce. As if a lifetime of success behind an office desk was made manifest in their soft white flesh. If there is one thing that proves that a man's perception of the world is entirely deluded, it is his ability to hold an image of himself as heroic while his body deteriorates.

I find this kind of fascination with mirrors strangely pleasing. It's as if my teachers from secondary school are still inside my unconscious mind flailing away. I give them voice and then I can't stop them, because this kind of psychological self-abuse is only the beginning; *was* only the beginning. I was alone and naked before the mirror, and on the edge of a great journey of self-discovery.

I was going to grasp my manhood again. I was going to pull my masculinity up from the floor, suck in my pot-belly and bend my head towards the great solitude wherein a man liberates his true self and becomes forever enlightened.

And besides all that, I was now my own master. I could do whatever I wanted. A man alone can please himself. He need pay no attention to manners, decorum or the various courtesies of living with another. I didn't have to talk to anyone in the jeep now. I could drive back to Leitrim listening to the radio. At night, I could move around the bed like a lazy bull, or a walrus, depending on how I felt. I could toss, turn and fart or scratch myself any way I wanted. In the evenings, I could put as much coal on the fire as pleased me. I could put far too much coal on the fire and no one would know as long as the chimney didn't burst into flames. And that hadn't happened yet. I could stack up the coal, the Polish doubles, so high in the grate that I would need to take off my clothes because of the heat. And I could do that too – take off my clothes. I could sit, strip, sweat, lean over the fire, drink wine, belch, watch *EastEnders*, *Doctor Who* or *Judge Judy*. Whatever I wanted. I could be obscene, vulgar or unconscious, without offending anyone. And in the mornings, I could put butter on my porridge and toss the bowl in the sink with the other dirty dishes; the pot and the wok and the cups and the plates from the previous night. I could go to my room, my writer's room, every day and close the door and not talk to another human being. I could reconnect with the wild man inside me; that brutish animal could sing in me without disturbance or without a sense of obligation to others.

But what if I couldn't? That thought had occurred to me. What if I was unable to endure being alone? The answer was simple. In fact, my security lay in the certitude that she would return. She wasn't going away for ever. I could safely play the Lone Ranger or the Buddha of Leitrim all day long with the knowledge that, even if I went completely daft, she would be home in just over a month and all would become normal again.

I wasn't jealous of her. Why would I be jealous? It's the last thing I would think of. She was an independent woman, an artist, and she was of course entitled to her own life. And what she did in Poland was her own business. She had been there a few times over the years. I knew she had friends in the Art School. I knew she always enjoyed

Warsaw, studying and working and talking about art and going to restaurants and museums.

So I let her off. Because I would do what a man does when he tears himself away from society and seeks out an isolated place like a bear seeks a solitary cave. I would do what the wild animal does when mother bear has moved down river, or when the beautiful woman bear has been swept up into the clouds by Ryanair. I would do nothing.

A GIRL FROM Latvia shouted 'room service', and knocked at the door three times between 11 a.m. and noon, eager to freshen the room for the next guest. So I phoned Reception and booked another night. That would give me twenty-four hours to recover from the drink, before driving into the Dublin traffic and negotiating the dual carriageway towards Blackrock and the bottlenecks running into the M50.

I phoned the Project Arts Centre and booked myself a ticket for *A Tender Thing*. The Project is one of my favourite theatres in Dublin. The Gate Theatre at the far end of O'Connell Street – once nicknamed Sodom because it was run by Micheál MacLiammóir and Hilton Edwards, Ireland's iconic gay men of the 1950s – is an elegant building, and I always love its frocked dramas. And then there is the Abbey Theatre, astutely nicknamed Begorrah because in every generation it rediscovers the argot of the Irish peasantry and stretches it to hyperbolic absurdity in the way that Irish audiences love – and which pleases the tourists, who come in summer and eat bars of chocolate as they watch the classics by O'Casey, Synge and J.B. Keane. But the Project Arts Centre always surprises me. It caters for young middle-classes, graduates of Trinity College and other sophisticates from the leafy suburbs who like a kind of erotic polish on their entertainment. Not for them the affected accents of nineteenth-century English heroines or the squalling agony of unrequited love among the peasantry. They present some dance theatre, and plays by lots of international writers and new interpretations of classics and there is no proscenium arch and I feel the players are reaching out to me with a wonderful intimacy.

So that's where I went. The play in question starred Olwen Fouéré and Owen Roe, two actors of superb abilities whom I knew at a slightly personal level from my own work in theatre.

A Tender Thing is about the enduring love of an elderly couple. The conceit is based on Romeo and Juliet's tragedy and, though the words are all Shakespeare, it presents its tale of love in a world of grim middle-aged reality. I was certain that it was my kind of play.

For the rest of the day, I lounged in the room, took a bath, went for a walk and messed about on Facebook. Just after 6 p.m., I headed for town. The weather forecast was for a dry night, though storms were expected at the weekend. But, being from Leitrim, I never trust weather forecasts so I faced the night in full battle dress – black plastic leggings, a yellow fisherman's raincoat and a weatherproof hat with a wide rim. I was hoping to have noodles in a cheap restaurant in Temple Bar just across the road from where the beloved once had a sculpture studio and where we used to dine long ago when we had no money. In those days, Temple Bar was a rundown labyrinth off Dame Street and the cobbled streets were usually empty. The buildings were derelict, apart from artists who rented big nineteenth-century rooms with holes in the floor. There was a pub where busmen used to drink as they came off duty. And only one café. And then a noodle bar. But that of course was before the boom, when the buildings were refurbished and shop fronts were cheered up and new restaurants opened and Temple Bar became the clichéd Artistic Quarter in every Dublin tourist brochure. And there were fewer artists because they couldn't afford the rents. Like me and the beloved, most of them fled to the west of Ireland long before the stag groups from the north of England began to every weekend to drink themselves into a stupor.

The noodle shop had closed down, while the beloved's workshop had been transformed into a flashy gallery, with a young man with a guitar stood in the doorway singing. Foregoing the noodles, I went into a fancy coffee house farther down the street with two long tables where young couples were chatting over lattes and green teas. I decided to sit by the window on a high stool, and kept my eye on the street. It was still early enough; the waves of women wearing fancy hen costumes and furry pink tiaras would sweep the street later in the evening. But, at 7 p.m., restaurants were still offering early bird menus to the few young backpackers who wandered the cobbled streets like lost chickens.

'I'll bring it over,' the man behind the counter said, and when he did it was warm but not hot, like I think a latte ought to be. I didn't have the courage to challenge him. And it's funny the way anxiety can build from that single thread into a great tapestry of negative emotion. I felt like any countryman feels on the sophisticated streets of a city; like an elderly gobshite. Public affection, kissing on the street, wandering aimlessly, sucking ice creams, sitting on steps or rolling loose cigarettes are all activities we associate with young people. It's just never something older people do. It's as if the high streets and shopping centres and culture quarter of modern cities are the playgrounds of late-developing adolescents. And it's no place for old men. And I felt I should not have brought my leggings and rain gear. I looked like a fisherman from the windy end of Killybegs. And when I tried to take the gear off, I felt everyone was staring as if I was undressing. So I sipped the cold latte and already felt a kind of defeat spreading across my skin.

Not that anyone was looking at me. They were far too interested in each other. In fact older people are invisible to the young. I was just experiencing the straightjacket of self-obsession that people get trapped in when depression is overwhelming them. When it becomes acute, some people can't go out the door. They don't want to be seen. They can't walk down a street. They think everyone is looking at them.

I even debated with myself about whether or not I was in the right mood for theatre. I might run into people I didn't want to speak with or people I knew who would look at me and see how I have deteriorated. So perhaps I shouldn't go. Perhaps I should flee back to the hotel.

When I looked out the window, I saw young Italian students with soft skin and dark olive eyes in furry anoraks holding each other. I saw a circle of tall Spanish girls, chattering like wild flamingos, their long noses like beaks, and enormous Picasso eyes darting here and there, and I saw a few drunk boys sheltering under the canopy of an Italian restaurant, gawking with the confused lust of meerkats. Not one of those people could care that I existed. And if I had been still suffering from depression, all this would have triggered an irrational panic, a fear that if I was to step onto that street every eye would turn to judge me in some negative way. But not any longer. I was a man who had been healed. A man who was on a spiritual journey.

So I went to the play despite my inhibitions, and it was beautiful. I cried all through it and when it was over, I wanted to go up and hug the actors. But that's where I drew the line. After all, I didn't know them very well.

And the one I might have hugged wasn't there; she was in a far country drinking vodka or sleeping soundly in her little cot in some tiny but warm room in the middle of Warsaw, while outside her window it was probably snowing. And I was alone in a strange crowd wrapped in the unpleasant delusion that the entire world might be out to get me. I slipped out of the theatre and stood on the street trying to get into my rain gear, and the texture of the raincoat made me feel like an insect in its shell.

I walked for forty minutes down Baggot Street, into Ballsbridge and towards the security of my hotel bedroom where I watched *Tonight With Vincent Browne* on the television. He was talking about the economy with a panel of academic and political experts. Two university professors with baggy cream jackets, PhDs in Economics and flamboyant neckties were pouring scorn on the stupidity of Irish politicians. And two politicians, a woman with alarmingly red lips and a boyish TD with red hair,

39

big ears and a suit that was far too small for him were both grinning. They stuck out their chins and smiled as if they were enduring bad wind.

The politics didn't interest me and I began to regret leaving the theatre so soon. Perhaps I should have gone for a drink with some of the cast. Perhaps I might have met some amazing young actress. She might have said, 'Do I know you?'

And I would have feigned false modesty and said, 'Oh, I don't think so. I don't live in Dublin anymore.'

And she would have said, 'Are you a writer?'

I would have maintained my façade of humility hoping that if I hung around long enough she might drink too much and then throw herself at me. On the other hand, I might have met some beautiful woman who seemed interested in me until she addressed me by another name and it would dawn on me that she thought I was someone else. I hate it when someone says, 'I love your work,' and then after two or three drinks you realise they have mistaken you for another writer. So maybe I was right to leave the theatre, I told myself. Maybe I am always right to shun the public world, because it never works out. I am condemned to a life of solitary confinement with a television set.

I suppose everyone has bad nights like that, when we are overpowered by a voice harassing us from the mirror. 'You stupid gobshite,' the voice says as we look at ourselves in bleak wonderment. That's what was happening. The black psychic dog within me was awake again. The cesspool of negative emotion that I personified as my own private Dracula and who sucked all energy out of my soul had returned. The negative voice, the talking fish, was coming my way, like a big pike through the muddy water with its teeth bared.

Once upon a time, there was an old priest in Cork. He suffered from low self-esteem. He got stressed when he had to preside at First Holy Communions. But one year, his parish was chosen to lead the Corpus Christi procession through the city. Hundreds of thousands of devout onlookers lined the streets as the procession passed. There were bands in uniform, and women in white veils, and children with baskets of rose petals, and choirs singing hymns, and at the centre of it all was the golden canopy, held by four posts firmly in the hands of four members of An Garda Síochána, and, under the canopy, the little priest held the monstrance wherein the sacred presence of God is made manifest in the white wafer host. This tiny piece of bread is the dramatic focal point of the entire Corpus Christi procession, and the old priest was terrified that he might let the monstrance slip. He clutched it ferociously and stepped carefully forward to the beat of a drum. And then suddenly the curate came rushing to his side and whispered in his ear, 'We forgot to put the host in the monstrance.'

The old priest winced. 'Fuck it,' he hissed, 'we always forget something.'

At least I woke up sober. I showered at 8 a.m. and went for another walk into town. All my negativity of the previous night was forgotten. As if it had never happened. As if it had was someone else's life. And I felt alive. Joyful. Exuberant. I could hardly contain myself as I cracked the shell of my boiled egg at breakfast in the dining room. I couldn't resist a second egg, and then pancakes. I thanked the young Lithuanian girl who served me coffee as if I had just been married to her the day before and was overwhelmed to see her so radiant on the first fine morning of our honeymoon. It was going to be a wonderful day.

At that moment, I felt especially delighted to know that the beloved was safely embedded in Warsaw and I had before me six weeks of solitude in which to drill into my deep unconscious, to examine the core of my psyche, to meditate myself into some great transcendent state of bliss in the hills above Lough Allen. But not before a walk into the city.

So I walked as far as the Apple store near Grafton Street because I needed a new charger for my phone and then I went up to Stephen's Green, where I sat on a seat watching a high-booted woman in a snug black coat having a video chat on her phone with someone in Spain. At least I think it was Spain because she was speaking Spanish. It might have been Mexico or Thailand for all I know. But I knew enough about Buddhism to realise that she and I were one. We were the one being. We shared a single core. Even the person in Mexico that was chatting to her in Spanish was just another part of the one we all were. The high-booted woman had raven-black hair, but nonetheless she could be a child of mine. She could be my mother. How wonderful that we were all so connected! As my therapist might have said, I was getting over-excited.

I treated myself to a pastry on Baggot Street.

'Would you like jam or cream with your scone?' she asked me.

'Could I have both?' I wondered.

'Of course,' she said, and jotted something on the notepad that was slung from the belt around her waist.

'Would you like it hot?'

'What?'

'The scone.'

'Oh, yes. Hot. I like it hot.'

And it came hot, with cream, and the coffee was hot.

Then a woman came in with a buggy. She had three children clinging to it and she struggled to negotiate her way around the tables. There was only one table free and it was beside me. She reached it and lifted an infant from the buggy. She put the three children around the empty table with the buggy and then she sat down at my table.

'Do you mind if I sit here for a minute?' she asked.

She was about thirty-five, blue-eyed and had blonde

43

hair as straight and clean as someone on Scandinavian television.

She ordered three fresh fruit drinks and a coffee for herself. And I was beginning to fantasise. She might have a very busy day ahead. Walking the two big ones to their school. Walking the little one to a crèche. Walking around the streets for hours with a baby in the buggy, shopping just to pass the time before returning to the crèche.

'Isn't it a lovely morning!' I declared, even though the strands of her blonde hair hanging over her nose were wet from the drizzle.

'Yeah,' she said, looking at me for the first time, with a certain curiosity.

'What I mean is,' I said, 'it would be lovely if it wasn't raining.'

'Right,' she said, nodding emphatically and then turning to her little ones at the other table playing games on mobile phones.

What I had meant to say was that it's a wonderful morning when I can get up in the fullness of my health, walk the city streets among the sauntering women, the jogging women, with their earphones plugged in, and the ones who dream and gaze and pass me by without the slightest glance. It's still wonderful. That's what I meant. But I didn't say it.

'You have your hands full,' I said.

'Don't talk to me,' she said. 'And I'm desperate for Garth

44

Brooks tickets. And they're queuing halfway down Grafton Street.'

Christ, I thought, *this is the great thing about cities. People talk to each other. They sit down with strangers and share intimacies.* Now I knew quite a lot about her. I knew she liked Garth Brooks. I knew she was even thinking of going to his concert. *Maybe she's trying to tell me something*, I thought. *Maybe it wasn't an accident that she sat down here.* After all, why did she not sit down with the other three at the other table? There was plenty of space. Maybe she unconsciously wanted distance between herself and the children for a moment. She needed to breathe as an individual and not as a mammy. And maybe she was drawn to me unconsciously. Maybe this is the moment wherein my life changes.

I felt like saying, 'Do you want me to go and queue for you? You can just sort out the kids and I'll meet you at lunchtime in Bewley's. I'll get you all the tickets you want.'

But I didn't. I knew that on the bipolar wheel, my emotions were on the crest. So I restored myself to reality.

'Oh,' I said. 'Garth Brooks. Yeah. He's a great singer.'

She smiled at me. Looked into my eyes. She was soft and emotional and because of the baby on her lap, she seemed full of maternal love. Maybe this was Mia Farrow and I was Woody; although I reminded myself how that turned out, which grounded me slightly.

But yet, I was looking into her eyes. Somewhere inside

45

me little happy juices were squirting out excessive doses of bliss, and I was contemplating how wonderfully open city people can be in the morning. I was convinced that I could tell if the dreams of any customer sitting at one of the tables near me were good or bad or if their sex was wild or mediocre by just looking into their eyes. And I was looking at everyone, and staring at the woman across the table from me.

I was thinking maybe I shouldn't go home at all. Maybe I should stay here in Dublin, this city throbbing with life. That's the thing I cling to as I get older – life. And there was life here. Maybe I should go to Garth Brooks. I was thinking maybe this woman at my table with her three baby bags full of wipes, bottles and Pampers is just waiting for me to say something. Maybe I should just say, 'Tell me what you dreamed of last night.'

But I didn't have time because all of a sudden he arrived – her husband or partner or whatever, presumably the father of her four children. And by the black woollen coat on him and the two pigskin gloves in one hand and the smell of his aftershave, I could see he wasn't stuck for a penny.

He sat at the table with the children. They all clambered around him with stories. And she, the Scandinavian television presenter, swooned and said, 'Ohhhhh, great! You're here!' And she moved over to the space her children were making for her at the other table and midway between the two tables his lips touched her cheek.

46

'I've got the car,' he said, like he was Colin Firth. 'And Susan is fine for Thursday with the kids. So we're free.'

And I wasn't even jealous of him because he did look a bit like Colin. He too was part of me. In the great oneness of the cosmos, and the oneness of the morning, he was only another part of the great oneness inside me. We were all one. That was the point I kept telling myself. In fact, maybe he was indeed Colin Firth. Maybe he actually was himself, and she was some old friend and he was bringing her to Italy for a break. Maybe she had cancer and he had flown in that morning out of compassion. 'And Susan is fine for Thursday with the kids.' So that was great! They were fine. They were free. How wonderful. I could share their joy. I wasn't one of those people who phone into radio talk shows to complain about the world; someone who would object to Susan and Colin and herself with her lovely babies driving around in a fancy car. *Maybe they have a house in Leitrim*, I thought. *Maybe they're going up there for the weekend, to their modest little cottage in the hills.* And who knows, they might like to meet other people like themselves; blow-ins as we're called in rural Ireland. Should I lean across and say, 'Excuse me. I'm sorry for interrupting, but you're not by any chance going to Leitrim?'

And he would turn to me, and then I'd know it was Colin Firth and he'd say, 'By jove, yes we are. We have a little cottage up there that we got for a song, but we don't know where to go for the fishing.'

47

'Ahh-ha,' I would reply, 'I'm so glad you asked. You see, I too live in Leitrim and my wife is away and of course you must come for dinner.'

'How spiffingly wonderful,' Colin might say. And we'd all be friends and have a great old weekend.

These fantasies almost unbalanced me. I spilled half my coffee on the table and so I decided to get back out onto the street and start walking before I did more damage than a bull in a china shop.

Thirty minutes later, I was almost at my hotel. The jeep was under the trees at the corner of the car park. I could see from a distance that it had been drenched with bird shit.

I paid the bill, went out to the jeep, brushed the bird shit off the windscreen, threw my luggage in the back, turned on the ignition and asked the sat-nav to show me the way home.

HEADING BACK to Leitrim, I was thinking of the fifty-inch television set sitting in the front room of our cottage. It's so big that we couldn't find a table to accommodate it. In fact, we didn't even buy it. It was a gift from a relation. And when a big television set comes out of the back of a van, you can't really say no. We just succumbed to the irresistible condition of being Irish.

Everyone in Ireland watches television. We're addicted to the sense of reality that it provides. Television seems real and more clear than ordinary life. People go to football matches, but they come home early from the pub to see what the game was like on television. During the boom, people used to spend Sunday mornings in Harvey Norman and Currys where there were electrical sections dominated by walls of large television sets. Televisions mounted on sleek black stands, with separate speakers on either side. Men would edge up to them and touch the screens like devout monks touching the tabernacle, knowing that within were all the digital paraphernalia to manifest the ultimate truth, to screen the world in all its deep reality, to show things not just as they are to human eyes but in their essence, in high definition.

And all because we lost faith in God, and in the foggy world of metaphysical reality.

The material realm became our truth. In rural Ireland people built houses that would have sufficed as palaces for Arabian princes, majestic castles on the sad little drumlins, and began driving around the pot-holed roads of the nation in BMWs and top-of-the-range 4x4s. The ground of human existence was established in tangible things. It was imperative that everything was real. Even the clarity of Tony Soprano's wife's lips when she was putting on her gloss required high definition. Sometimes I suspect that it was faith in high definition that encouraged the fashion among some women to eradicate pubic hair with fancy little pink razors, as a sort of assurance that the vagina itself was also a material certainty.

Myself and the beloved missed the excesses of the Celtic

Tiger. We lived in a cottage and we couldn't find a place where the enormous television would fit without one end of it blocking a door or masking a window. So we positioned it at an angle, between the fireplace and the glass door into the sunroom. I say 'we', but it was me that wanted it.

And I am wondering as I drive, why am I addicted to television? Why do I have a television the size of a small cinema screen? Something that is so out of proportion to the size of the house that it is impossible to be in the room for a single moment without being aware of it. I can't answer this except to say that sitting down with the beloved to watch soap operas was always a way of entering deeply into her presence. The fact that the programme was vacuous and devoid of any meaning made it an even deeper experience for us. It was like entering the great bliss void together, like watching flames flickering in the fire hundreds of years ago.

I suppose there's very little to do in rural Ireland, at the top of a mountain on a winter night.

This is something that urban people can never understand. They ask me at dinner tables if I watch television, and I go on for longer than is necessary, exalting the pleasures of Home Box Office dramas, and they sniff and say, 'How interesting,' as if I was talking about a zoo in China. When I'm finished, someone flips a comment in front of me like a dagger. 'Of course, we never watch television.' And that ends that. But they don't know what it's like to live up a mountain.

But it's not just televisions that we need. Country people listen to the radio all day with a collective intensity that marks them out from city dwellers. They listen morning, noon and night. They stop what they're doing, they stand still with a dishtowel in the hand or they put down the razor or they become transfixed at the fire grate holding a coal scuttle just to hear the next sentence that the person on the wireless might utter.

'Did you hear that?' some man says, coming into the kitchen to address his wife, because there's always more than one radio in any house.

In the kitchen, there is often a big old-fashioned wireless, the one that got thrown out of the sitting room when the first television arrived. A big bulky box of art deco panels with a glowing glass window and a dial that spins across the medium waves. And in the living room, there might be something more contemporary; twin speakers on either side of a wifi adapter perhaps, with a cradle and socket to connect an iPod or iPad, and which might transmit all the radio stations in the world. But there are usually radios upstairs too, in the bedrooms. €30 worth of vulgarity from discount stores, made in China, silver-coloured lumps of plastic shining like the dashboard of a Korean jeep with a transistor inside that can only pick up RTÉ or Shannonside or Galway Bay FM or whatever the local radio station in the district is. Which is what everyone wants. If something was said and you missed it then you would be the only one in the supermarket queue who couldn't comment on it. And maybe you'd feel like you had missed something. The details of their funerals read out in solemn tones with soft music in the background to soothe the listeners; the women toiling at the sink in tears, and the men at the dinner table with broken hearts.

Radio provides a focus, an object for unconscious anger and other emotions that may arise. Like the child who is bullied in school and then goes to his bedroom and pulls off his teddy bear's ears, there is nothing more dangerous than a man pent up with a rage that has festered from some abuse or humiliation that was never acknowledged. And it's easy for a wife to become the negative 'other' who carries the can for such a man's wounds. In Ireland, hurt is the default condition of the psyche. We are marked by a sense of victimhood, and a foggy wound that is linked backwards to the Famine, to oppression by the British, to the tyranny of nuns and priests, and forwards into all possible situations in the future wherein we may be hurt. That's what we listen for. We are not really listening to the radio. We are monitoring our own unconscious. We are waiting to be annoyed.

And the minute we are annoyed, we take up the telephone. 'Did you hear that bastard on the radio? Wasn't he outrageous? I'm so upset. I think I'll phone *Liveline* this afternoon.' And on it goes for hours or days.

The indignation of the people becomes sulphuric. We

suck up the hurt, nurture the wound and relish the pain. We rise for a moment out of our unconscious soup of jigs and reels because we have been offended. We have been wronged again. And so we remain hopelessly addicted to our little receivers.

I suppose we say so little of any meaning to each other face to face that we need someone else to expose emotions. We talk at each other in a manner that Freud once described as the ability to say nothing by saying everything, and then we switch on the radio to hear pain expressed, depression revealed, anxiety and orgasms gushing over the airwaves at us. And we love it. And if a woman is weeping at the sink while chopping the carrots or if a man is swallowing rage with every bite of his rasher while he sits to his tea with the evening news, it is a private affair.

'Your eyes are red, my darling. Were you crying?'

'Oh, no,' she protests, 'I was only chopping onions.'

We talk about nothing by talking about everything. And in the countryside people who are isolated cannot bear to look at the blowing rain, or hear the keening wind across all the bleak bogs and flooded fields. So they listen to the radio. Single men with cupboards full of tablets listen. Unmarried brothers who once courted the same woman listen. Spinsters who live on sliced ham and wrinkled lettuce leaves from their own gardens listen.

My mother used to put the radio on at night when she was going to bed. Her favourite station was the BBC World

Service. She would put it on at full volume and it remained so until morning. Whenever I stayed with her, during her later years, I would try to sleep in the room next to hers, awake until maybe 4 a.m., listening to correspondents from the Sudan and Nigeria discussing crop failures, threats of drought and the ongoing casualties of war.

I asked her once why she kept it on. She said it helped her sleep. I think what she meant was that when the radio was on, she could hear nothing else. She wasn't vulnerable to disturbing sounds in the night that might frighten her. If someone broke into the house, she wouldn't know about it unless the robbers came upstairs and asked her to turn down the volume.

Myself and the beloved were not strictly speaking addicted to television. For there were many nights when we never turned it on at all. Hundreds of nights when she sat by the fire sketching or fingering her iPad or knitting, and I sat there at the opposite side of the fire, both of us cramped on dainty little armchairs and huddled towards the flames, because the house is so small, with our backs to the monstrous television set and I would just gaze at her in awe, and be amazed at how she could knit.

I was driving past the turn for Maynooth, thinking how wonderful it was that an academy once as intellectually stimulating as a wardrobe of dead flies had finally been transformed into a real university, bristling with young students. I imagined what it might be like to saunter

55

through the gates again towards the library, now probably full of beautiful young women and not the sad, pale-faced clerics who had sat there with me on creaking chairs reading books about Thomas Aquinas. And then suddenly the jeep drifted across two lanes as I daydreamed, and a car behind me blew his horn to get me out of the way.

THE ROAD TO Leitrim is straight and bypasses most towns, but I left the N4 at the Roosky exit because I wanted to visit an old friend, a long-black-haired poet whose wife was expecting a baby in the coming days. Both of them were at home and I went in and joined them for a pot of tea, and I said, 'The beloved has gone to Poland.'

He was watching television. She was in the bedroom.

He said, 'You will miss her.'

I agreed.

His long black hair was tied with an elastic band at the nape of his neck and he wore silver rings on his thumb and forefinger as he rolled a joint.

'I feel fragile,' I said. 'I hope to do a bit of meditation when I'm alone in the house. I had this notion that I'd set up a nice secure nirvana, a solitude of calm abiding, and just sit watching the grass grow for a month. But now that she's gone, I'm wondering if that is just a fantasy.'

'Sure, she'll be back in a couple of weeks, man. Relax. You're fretting too much.'

'I know.'

'You'll have a great time on your own,' he said. 'You'll have a chance to check out things inside yourself. And don't be afraid to go in there.'

'In where?' I asked.

He pointed to his head.

'Get in there, man. Take the opportunity to go inside.'

I'm always alarmed when people begin talking like they were in an episode of *Star Trek*.

'I'll probably just sit on my arse for six weeks,' I muttered.

'Anyway,' he said, 'you're looking good. You've lost weight.'

'But there's another issue,' I said.

'What's that?'

'I get frustrated with myself. I think I have become domesticated.'

'How do you know you're domesticated?'

'I got slippers for Christmas,' I replied. 'With a tartan pattern.'

'Man,' he said, 'that's not good.'

His wife emerged from the bedroom, a woman with long sandy hair, wearing a sleeveless dress of rainbow colours down to her ankles. I couldn't resist staring at her long, elegant toes as they peeped out from under the dress and flapped about in brown leather sandals. He asked me if I wanted another cup of tea.

She had been doing yoga in the bedroom, she said, and now she was going out for air. She looked at his smoking cigarette with sadness. I kissed her on the cheek, as a sort of hello and goodbye, and wished her well. He got up and hugged her too. 'Love ya, baby,' he muttered, and held the door for her as she went out into the world like a goddess to bless the cosmos or water the plants. When she was gone, we both sat in silence staring at the door. The room felt completely empty. He asked me again if I wanted another cup of tea, but I refused.

I continued on towards Carrick-on-Shannon and then to Drumshanbo where I stopped at the Gala shop to get some shopping, and finally out the Drumkeerin road, and up the narrow lane we call the mountain road, beyond the dirty sheep, the hungry horses and the abandoned thatched studio that two Hungarian artists once lived in before they fled to lower ground on the other side of the lake where they set up a ceramic studio. I could see the wind turbines up ahead near Spion Kop. Each year, there are more blades. More pillars of white reaching into the sky, confusing the hen harriers. They sneak them up on great transporter vehicles at night when people are asleep.

When I arrived at the cottage, I parked the jeep and I said hello to the cat, who was flinging insults at me for abandoning her overnight, and I went inside and shovelled out the ashes and put a flaming firelighter under six briquettes. I was lucky. There were only three matches left in the box.

I checked Facebook a few times to see if she was online. There were a few new additions; pictures of Warsaw taken from inside a train and one of her friends smiling at an art exhibition. So, I concluded that she had access to wifi. I tried messaging her, but the icon beside her name on Facebook said she was offline.

Well, OK. That was fine. By now, the fire was blazing and I sat back on the sofa with the cat to watch the two last episodes of *Breaking Bad* although I kept one eye on my Facebook page in case any signal came in from Warsaw.

Eventually I couldn't resist a text.

I'm back in the house. The cat is happy. All seems fine.

I sent it twice. But it didn't deliver. She had turned off her phone.

When I woke the following morning, I had forgotten her. It was 8 a.m. and the sun had just then risen above the slope of the mountain and was like an orange ball of fire in the chilly grey sky.

My first emotion was one of surprise that the sun was orange, and that it was shining through the cream curtains. I felt like a child long ago who had been allowed to stay home from school. I could lie there all day just watching the clouds being pushed across the sky and be happy in myself thinking of how far I had come in life. When I was a child, I used to see Warsaw on the dial of the old radio and when I twirled the knob so that the needle pointed to it I could hear the sound of a man talking in a strange language behind the crackling static, though I didn't know what the word 'Warsaw' meant. And now I had ended up married to a wonderful artist who was at that very moment walking the streets of that extraordinary city. I thought about the BBC too, and the splendid gift it is to live in a world where I can press the app on my iPhone and hear the soft fluttering violas of unnamed musicians in a London studio being broadcast on *Breakfast* on Radio 3. It would have all been perfect if she had been beside me.

But there were obstacles too. When I got up and went to the kitchen, I realised that I had forgotten to get milk in the shop. In fact, I had forgotten to get bread, coffee, marmalade and even tablets for the dishwasher. She had actually said it in the hotel – 'Don't forget milk on your way home.' It's one of the great gifts women have. They can anticipate what you might need in a domestic situation. And men hate that. They don't like being told things that make them feel incompetent. Of course they *are* incompetent. It's just they don't like to admit it. And it's staggering how irritated a man can get when a woman says those simple words: 'Don't forget the milk.'

Of course I won't forget the milk, he thinks. *Does she suppose I'm stupid? Does she think I'm incapable of keeping the kitchen organised?*

'I'm a modern man,' he insists. 'Some of my best friends are feminists.' And he stares around the kitchen convinced that if he ever bothered doing the housework, he would of course do it far better than her. But I'm not that bloated with hubris. It's just that we live five miles from a shop and so it's not funny to forget. And I was going around from one press to another muttering, 'Where did she leave the sugar?'

No.

'Where did she hide the sugar?'

No.

'For fuck's sake, where is the fucking sugar?'

The bottom line was that there didn't seem to be any sugar. I had no choice but to drink a bitter black coffee, and skip the refinements of porridge, toast or marmalade. It wasn't a great start. But it reminded me that there were other issues. Like which bin was due to go out on Friday. I couldn't remember if it was the blue one or the black one that had gone out last time.

I knew that with the dishwasher not functioning because we were out of tablets, the kitchen would soon back up with dirty plates and cups. And I wasn't going to start hand-washing them all. And then I couldn't find the mop to clean up the cold coffee that had spilled straight out on the floor when I opened the lid of the coffee pot because I didn't think there was any coffee in it. How was I to know that the pot was still half full of cold coffee? Doesn't someone usually clean it before they go to bed? Yes? Well, there you go. So I made a note of that for future reference.

But I was still looking for the mop. I tried the scullery, the shed, outside the back door, behind the fridge. *Where the fuck is the mop?* I wondered. I was getting exhausted and it was only 8.30 a.m.

Maybe I need to relax, I thought. Go out to my room and chill. Leave everything as it is for the moment. Go to town at lunch and pick up stuff. I could make a list of 'stuff'. That's the trick. That's what women do. They make a list. That's what my mother used to do. She'd have a list every Friday for me. Even if her mind was dissolving when she was in her late eighties, she always had her list.

So I made another coffee and took it out to my studio. I crossed the back yard with the laptop in one hand and the coffee and my keys in the other. It was raining and the rain splashed into the mug. I ran to the patio door, fiddled with the keys, almost dropped the computer, opened the door, and then spilled half the coffee as I went inside. And for fuck's sake, what was sitting on the desk from two days earlier? The sugar bowl.

At least now I was getting into better form because I was in my refuge. My shed. My isolated study where no one bothers me. And there were two firelighters left in the packet. The lake stretched before me. I cleaned out the ashes from the stove, placed the firelighters between two turf briquettes and set them on fire. Then I settled into a swivel chair to contemplate the day.

It's not just a phrase I picked up from some cheap self-help book about Buddhism. It's what Pabongka Rinpoche said in his book *Liberation in the Palm of Your Hand*. And he's the real deal. He's the bee's knees. You won't find him on YouTube. He didn't waste his time doing videos for the internet. Of course he's long dead but the book is still out there.

The mind is like an elephant, he said.

He would have heard the same phrase from his teachers when he was a young student in some remote Tibetan monastery. It's an image commonly used for the unruly mind in lots of Tibetan texts on mind training. The elephant goes where it wants. And there's no telling when an elephant will change its mood. There's no guiding it or tying it down, unless you use the ropes of meditation and mind training at which Pabongka Rinpoche was apparently such an adept.

My mind is like a particularly dysfunctional elephant. My mind is like an elephant that has escaped from traumas in a circus. My mind is like an elephant that might drag me off a cliff at any moment in a sudden fit of rage. Such is the state of my mental disequilibrium that I am a victim every morning to what rises up in my mind, and I have utterly no control over it; as my teacher once said to me when we were in Mongolia together, 'Always something arising – but never what you expect.'

I couldn't have expected what came into my mind that morning when I knelt down on the floor of my studio to meditate. It wasn't the beloved. It wasn't the episodes of *Breaking Bad* I had watched the night before. It wasn't what food I planned to put on the list before going to town. It wasn't even the cat, though she was at the window, screaming to be allowed in (and just by the way, I was out of cat food as well). But none of these things disturbed me.

It was my mother who came, like a ghost flitting in and out of my mind, like something in the distance, like a small moth in the corner of my eye at first, or in the back of my mind, as they say. She was in the back of my mind but I certainly noticed her there.

This is how it happens. Sometimes we live through

moments of intensity like a death, and it's so overwhelming that we replay the moment over and over again. We can smell it and touch it repeatedly in our mind. And then one day, the event arises as usual, but it's different. We see it in a new light. And there is no reason for this. It just happens.

When my mother died, I was with her. And her going away from the world was simple and eloquent. She panted her way as if she were taking giant steps, one at a time towards a summit. And when she reached the summit, she vanished.

I had replayed that moment over and over again in the two years since she died. I can still remember sitting on an armchair at the wall just inside the door of her room in the nursing home. Sometimes I would get up and stand at the foot of the bed. I remember a radio in the distance, out on the corridor, and what music was playing in the very moments when she stopped breathing. But what never occurred to me until that morning, sitting in a swivel chair in my studio, the cat outside the window, the beloved in Poland, two years after my mother had died, what had never occurred to me until that moment was that I had not held her. And it horrified me, like a letter that announces some terrible debt you owe and just falls through the letterbox and lands on the floor at your feet. I never held her. OK, there might have been a moment when I engaged her in a chilly embrace akin to what the pope might offer another fully vested bishop during the

66

sign of peace at mass; a fumbling formality without much passion. But that is not the way I held the beloved. Not the way I held the cat. Not the way I held my own child when first I took her from the cot in the hospital delivery room. Not that way. I never held my mother like that. And she was obliged to go, to leave, to head down along the long, dark tunnel of death without a human hug from me. My brother was there and he treated her beautifully. He hugged and held and blessed and kissed her. But I just watched. From me she went away empty-handed, empty-armed. And there is nothing so empty as the beginning of a journey when you have not been fortified by the assuring hug of someone you love.

Even at her funeral, I had felt unbearably sad without understanding why.

I stood by the graveside, realising that I could have treated her far better. I could have loved her more or said something to heal the unsaid things of a lifetime. I could have even offered my heart, openly, and said, 'Mammy, I do love you. I always have.' I could have done kind things more often, especially at the end. Just to make her smile. And I could have done more to make her life easier. But I didn't. And I only realised all this after she was gone.

I remember getting out of the black car just behind the hearse as it arrived at the graveyard and feeling suddenly distressed by the crowds standing around, looking at the coffin as it was slid out of the hearse. With my brother and cousins, I put my shoulder to the grim timber box and we negotiated our way up the hill on a narrow path that led through other graves and tombstones, until we were at the place where my father had been buried forty years earlier. It was a path she had travelled well each summer to put flowers on his grave and stand bewildered with a little beret on her head as the priests blessed the graves, when hundreds of people from Cavan squashed together around their family plots to remember their dead.

A black slab declares my father's dates of birth and death. Halfway down the smooth limestone are the words: 'The Lord is my Shepherd, there is nothing I shall want', which is what my brother and I had agreed was sufficient at the time. But our mother insisted without us knowing that a further phrase be added, so that in its entirety the slab now reads: 'The Lord is my Shepherd, there is nothing I shall want – erected by his sons.'

I smiled when I saw it again as her coffin rested on a platform of crossbeams astride the empty hole in the plot where she would soon be planted.

The priest said his prayers. The relations and old friends shaded their eyes from the July sun and mumbled a decade of the rosary beneath dramatic tufts of cloud. And that was it. A blustery summer day. Strong showers and intermittent blasts of sunlight. My mother was in her grave.

An old man who had known her well grabbed me by the elbow so suddenly that I almost fell into the black hole.

68

'How are you now?' he enquired.

'I'm fine, Mr Dolan,' I replied, because as a child I had only known him by his surname.

'Well, your mammy is gone to a better place,' he declared.

Mr Dolan was old now but I remembered him from those Friday afternoons when I was six and I used to go shopping with Mother. He worked in a grocery shop on Main Street. He had long wavy blond hair back then, and a blue tie, and he was the one who had a stylish way of wrapping the ham in brown paper and then slipping the white twine around it and cutting the twine with a tug of his fingers, which always amazed me. He would present the parcel of cold ham to my mother and wink at me, or give me a mint sweet from the big jar with the image of the polar bear. But he too had grown old, and his face was skeletal. His hair had turned white, his blue tie wandered in the wind and his dentures were not firm in his gums; they floated about his mouth as he scrutinised me and leaned his enormous purple nose into my face as if he could smell my emotions. Everyone knew I had been sick. I had been depressed for a year or two, and it was no secret. But he sniffed me with an intimacy that made me feel ashamed.

'I heard you went through a bit of a stormy patch last year,' he said.

'Yes,' I admitted, 'but it's over now.'

'Of course it is,' he agreed. 'Sure it happens to the best

69

of us. It's the interior weather. It's like everything else. It's unpredictable. One day sunshine and then a week of rain.'

He squeezed my elbow tightly once more.

'I'm sorry about your mother,' he said. 'But you need to mind yourself now.'

And suddenly he was gone. He dashed into the crowd as the crowd crushed in for my hand and mumbled their sympathy in my ear.

I kept up a show of grim cheerfulness throughout the funeral pageantry. But inside I was numb and brittle. I felt my depression might return at any moment. I suspected Dracula was standing under the rowan trees on the edge of the graveyard waiting to embrace me when I was alone.

'She was a big age,' someone said of Mother.

'She was ninety-six,' I replied.

'Sure it was time for her to go,' another one said.

'Aye.'

'She had a good innings.'

'She did.'

'She was a monument.'

'She was.'

And on it went for half an hour at the graveside. Old broken men and women huddling in a circle around the mound of clay; the last of her generation, the flowers that had bloomed when she had bloomed and were now waiting for their own time to face the dark. And me in my late fifties and no child left inside me to cry for Mammy anymore.

I tried to remember her dancing. Or at least, while I was standing at the grave, I tried not to visualise what she looked like in the coffin or to remember how gaunt and haggard she had become in the last hours of her life, inhaling every precious breath. That was too upsetting. And I tried to avoid listening to the shovels of mud clattering down on the coffin lid.

There were other things for me to consider. I was focusing on the house – Glenasmole – a semi-detached building on Farnham Road just outside Cavan town where she had lived for sixty years. A house that had been dark and stuffy for two years, since she went away to the nursing home. A house that someone now had to open up and examine and clean.

After a respectable amount of time standing at the grave, and shaking hands with friends and relatives, everyone drifted towards the Kilmore Hotel down the road from the sloping graveyard. I followed behind. But first I blessed myself and took one last look at the flowers on the grave. With my eyes closed, I bade her what I thought was a last farewell. Then I walked down the slope, reflecting to myself that she was beside her husband at last. The grave had been filled. The earth now lay in a heap of black clay, covered with a few wreaths. That was the end of it.

I went into the church to pray at the altar rails and I saw the priest in the sacristy, a boyish intellectual taking off his white vestments. I thanked him for speaking so kindly about her life during the mass that morning and I knelt for a moment at the railings where my mother and father had knelt on their wedding day in 1950. The circle was completed. And I made a mental note to get her name onto the headstone.

The atmosphere in the Kilmore Hotel was cheerful – there's only so much grief you can show for a woman who was almost one hundred years old when she died. It's more a sense of relief. There is a tendency to celebrate her life, as if the day was a festival. Recalling anecdotes that summed up her character. Having a few drinks and a hearty dinner of soup and roast beef and fat puddings, and enjoying the sense of being alive without her. There is always a sense of liberation and pleasure for mourners who are, at least for the moment, still over ground and capable of enjoying the taste of good whiskey.

'May she rest in peace,' we all agreed after every round.

I remember gazing out the window of the dining room in the Kilmore Hotel for a long time. I could see the graveyard. She was still that close. Her nephews and nieces drank pints of ale and glasses of whiskey after the meal, and their children ate crisps and ran around the sofas in the foyer. They embraced and hugged and all agreed that Nellie was the last of her kind, the last of the great characters in Cavan town. They agreed that she had had a long and healthy life, and that she had been lucky in love, and kind to strangers, especially those in trouble, and wasn't it a pity that she had to go so suddenly in the end. 'She was a saint,' they said in all sincerity. And later they said she was a rogue – 'a pure demon of a woman if you crossed her'. Distant relations took photographs on their phones and promised to meet again soon, and not just at the next funeral. There was a sense of relief that the day was almost over. The book was closed. Nellie Finlay was no more.

I was looking out the window at the tombstones glistening in the slanting sun and when everyone had gone away and I had paid the bill for the meal, I got into the jeep and drove in through town and out Farnham Road towards her house. Glenasmole.

There it was, just beside the General Hospital, on a hill called the Rock Cross. Four houses standing alone. There were signs of life in the other three but at Glenasmole the weeds were coming up through the tarmac. The avenue was overcome by trees and bushes on either side. I walked around the gable and entered by the back door. I suppose I still wasn't satisfied that I had bid her a final and complete farewell from my heart, because the pageantry of the funeral didn't allow me enough quiet reflection, and I thought her smiling face would be more intense in the house than at the graveside.

But now that she was buried, there was no meaning in the house. Her clothes didn't mean anything and the ornaments and objects she had gathered, hoarded and loved for fifty years, and crammed onto every mantelpiece and into every china cabinet in the house, were suddenly bereft of any further significance. There was no sense to what lay in the wardrobes upstairs or to the dishes on the drying rack beside the sink. While she was in the nursing home I had always convinced myself that it was only for a short while and that she would eventually return to her home. And everything in the house signified something to her and everything mattered to her. So I touched as little as possible.

'She's not dead,' I would tell myself, as if disturbing anything might have been an unkindly act.

But now that she was dead I was forced to face the clutter and jumble of old clothes and broken delph. I put the palm of my hand on the old storage heater in the hallway, and checked that it was cold. In the drawing room, I checked another heater. The room was stuffy. The windows had not been opened for a long time and the sun had blazed into the room through June and July. But the radiators were off, so that was fine. Then I went upstairs, a solid, carpeted stairway, though it creaked in the same places as it had done years before when I was coming home from carnivals as a teenager in the middle of the night and would want to reach my bed without waking either of my parents.

There was a musty smell on the landing and in the corridor. I tried to open the bathroom window but it almost fell apart, so I left it as it was.

It was my first time in the house since she had died

two days earlier, and I didn't want to hang around too long. But I was drawn to a chair. It was in the front room. A chair that I had bought for her five years earlier in McIntyre's Furniture World. At the time, she could not manage to get up out of the low, soft armchairs, and this one had a high seat and a straight back. In all other respects, it was a fine, soft, upholstered throne. But she always looked rigid in it and just before she went into the nursing home, she was beginning to have difficulty getting in or out of it. I remember being terrified each week when I was saying goodbye, in case she fell. She'd stand up, escort me to the hall and close the door behind me. Then she'd walk back to the front room and throw herself in the general direction of the chair. I'd be outside the window looking in. She'd aim her body at it and all I could do was stand there gawking and hope she wouldn't miss. If she missed and fell she'd break her hip, with me looking at her through the window.

But now I was looking at the chair. I could almost see her sitting there, and hear her speak, as she once spoke to me many years earlier, when I was in the pit of depression, and had come to her for some comfort.

'If you want to cry, go upstairs,' she'd said coldly, when tears threatened my face in that same room in 1979. I was twenty-six, a grown adult, and yet I craved for her to hold me. And for a moment, our eyes met and I saw in her a naked terror and I felt her helplessness. It was like a sound

75

coming from a closed room where she had lived alone and untouched for far too long. She could never have held me then. I could see that. She could never hold anyone again. Yes, she could still be held by other people; those who came to her door sustained her, those who met her in the supermarket and in the street, and the nurses, the doctor, the home help and all her friends, they all held her, and the world held her, and the routines of her life held her, like going to 10 a.m. mass every morning for years or making her porridge in the microwave before going to bed, so that all she had to do in the morning was press the button and reheat it. All those routines held her. It wasn't her fault that she could not hold me. She just wasn't able to do it. And realising that felt like some kind of intimacy.

Of course they say that men ought not to cry openly, but to me it has always seemed natural. I know men cry in public, with a kind of bravado or performance skill, at football matches and whenever they're watching rugby in a pub, but there is a reluctance to share tears in any intimate situation. They go out to the street and cry. They leave the room. They apologise. Even I prefer to cry alone. It's not something I like to do with someone staring me in the face, apart from my therapist. But over the years, I have certainly cried a lot, whether because of mental anguish, fear of the future or just as a result of something trivial on the television, like the sight of women in period costumes on BBC as they rise up in rebellion against Mr Darcy or other such patriarchs, with the surprise of larks. I often wonder what women would think of me if they knew that.

And I remember one occasion when I caught my old friend the General in tears, and I had to look away. I was getting water from the tap in his yard one afternoon just before New Year, during a cold spell. I'd noticed that the snow all about me was stained with blood, where they had shot a horse on Christmas Day.

'She slipped on the ice,' the General had said, 'and we could do nothing for her.'

His eyes had watered and he'd looked at the empty snow with such confusion that no one could doubt but that he had loved his mare.

And I remember the time foot and mouth swept the country and big farmers from Monaghan, Tyrone and the Cooley Peninsula had wept every evening on the television news like little boys. The camera would catch them standing in a gateway, with a stick in hand, and the field behind them full of beautiful beasts, black-and-white dairy cows, the descendants of cattle that had grazed the same fields decades earlier.

'My father had this herd, and his father before him,' the farmer would be saying. And then he would turn to take a glance at the field and he'd be broken. 'They'll all have to go,' he'd say, the words whispered and the tears welling and overflowing in his eyes. And their crying often made me cry.

I spent years wrapped in sorrowful lament, posing as a melancholic poet in my college days, affecting the airs of a devout saint in various churches in later years, and when alone I released myself with tears that would fill a lake. But as I gazed at my mother's chair, I felt like I had a stone in my chest and no matter what I touched I couldn't cry.

FOR THE FIRST month after my mother died in July 2012, I walked about the world with a new lightness. It's not something I admitted to anyone, but I felt a sense of exhilaration to be above ground when someone so solid and enduring as Mother was now no more. Then after a certain time, issues began to arise. Letters started coming in the door. There were all sorts of institutions that needed forms to be filled in and evidence submitted to establish that this person was now legally dead. Most importantly, her death certificate needed to be completed.

And then I needed to fill in forms in order to close her bank account and to close down her social welfare file and to repay the two weeks' pension that had inadvertently gone into her account on the day of her death and to close the account with the nursing home. And the solicitor wanted to know what was going to happen to the house. There were forms surfacing everywhere. But the house was the most important issue.

My mother had left the house to my brother and me in equal parts, but my brother intimated to me that he wanted to give me his share as a gift. I was moved by his generosity, and I accepted. But the house didn't feel like mine. Or his. It was still hers; a dark enclosure where she had brooded in silence for forty years.

The solicitor phoned and asked if I could deliver the death certificate as soon as possible so that they could sort out probate on her estate. I should pick it up at the register office, he said, which was in a small building at the gates of Cavan General Hospital and happened to be just across the road from Glenasmole. So a week after the funeral, I returned to Cavan, drove past the wrought-iron front gate, rusting at the sides and at all the joints, and saw the nameplate on which 'Glenasmole' was hardly visible because of the moss and green slime. In the register office, I spoke to a woman behind the counter and filled in the forms and got the certificate. Then I brought it to the solicitor's office, and that was an end of it.

But on the way home, driving past the house again and seeing its closed gate and vacant upstairs windows, I decided to go inside for no particular reason. It was my first visit since the day of the funeral and this time I decided to examine things in more detail.

From the sunroom at the back of the house I passed through the kitchen, a room she had insisted on carpeting about ten years before she died, because her feet got cold on the bare tiles. The Sacred Heart picture on the wall was faded and the ink scrawl that marked her husband's, her own and her children's names had been erased by time. A round tin of Roses chocolates sat on the table. But none of these things disturbed me.

In the drawing room, Pope Benedict XVI stared at me from a postcard on the mantelpiece; the German theologian leered out of the frame with eyes that my daughter had once observed were very creepy. But that didn't disturb me either.

His photograph was flanked by long-legged African birds, like herons, carved in black ebony. They had been brought from Nigeria in 1966 by Father Pat, a distant cousin.

There were pictures of 'the two boys', as she called me and my brother, in First Communion suits beside the birds. A bland landscape painting of an English meadow hung over the mantelpiece. An electric heater with fake flames behind dark glass was tucked into the fire grate. A small television sat on the coffee table in the opposite corner. A cream nightdress hung across the back of the high armchair. A bundle of Sunday newspapers lay on the floor, yellowed by two years of sunlight. The standard lamp under which my father had once read his books was still plugged in and a bookcase in which he had locked away his precious books stood in the corner. I peered through the glass and wondered where the key might be; not that there was much of interest in there apart from old Catholic apologists from the 1930s and a few accountancy volumes that he had read for his examinations many years earlier – and a long brown envelope containing his will. The sofa that no one had sat on for years was piled high with pillows, bed linen and nightdresses. The card table was dusty. It had come originally from my grandmother's house, a dull, broken antique that spent some years in a shed. Mother had had it restored by the Robinson brothers in Killeshandra and when she brought it home, she glowed with happiness to have such a memento of her own mother.

It was made of polished mahogany, a central stem branching into four delicate legs. The table itself was square, but could be folded to half its size, with drawers underneath for the cards. The drawers had eventually filled up with bottles of cough mixture, tablets, tubes of ointment for her legs, a white raincoat, a pack of cards and some rosary beads. And the table too had gathered dust for two years. The cream wallpaper was falling off the walls behind a drinks cabinet in the opposite corner, which she had taken from her brother Oliver's house when he died – though Oliver never drank in his entire life and I always thought it was an unusual memento by which to remember him. But he was an enormous figure in my mother's little world, and he had achieved great success as a civil servant, eventually becoming the secretary to three presidents. When I was a child, he was the benchmark of dignity, success and ethical standards in our family. He had lived alone in a semi-detached house on Croagh Patrick Road in Dublin, and I had marvelled at the timer on his cooker, which could trigger the hot plates at the stroke of noon to heat potatoes, and have them ready for his lunch when he walked in the door to the red Formica table in his little kitchen, a stone's throw from the president's residence.

Every summer, he had holidayed on the Aran Islands, speaking Irish and reading books. His feet had spread in his sandals and he found it difficult to get them back into the stiff shoe leather when his holiday was over and his presence was once again required on the lush carpets of Áras an Uachtaráin. Now he sleeps, enfolded in the arms of his own mother and beside his father on a slope in Cullies graveyard, side by side with girls who died in the Poor Clare Orphanage fire, and all the other remembered and unremembered heroes of Cavan town. I often drove Mother out to put flowers on his grave, close to where a new road has been cut through the drumlins and which

83

shortens the journey to Enniskillen and on which the traffic flows day and night, and trucks honk their horns and the noise is carried in the wind into the graveyard and across the tombstones of the resting dead.

In the hallway of Mother's house, the wallpaper was also in tatters from the dampness that had inched up behind it from year to year, and the floor, where I remember red and cream tiles in my childhood, had been carpeted with a dizzy paisley design on a cream background. A yellow two-bar electric heater sat idle at the first step of the stairs, sitting there since a care worker had noticed that the flex was frayed and had insisted on taking it away, so that it wouldn't cause a fire. Mother had thought she was robbing it, so the care worker had left it alone, where it remained for years. But none of that upset me.

I was uneasy about opening the dining-room door because, for two years, Mother had slept in there, when she could no longer negotiate the stairs, before finally surrendering to the prospect of ending her days in a nursing home.

The sideboard on the left was cluttered with wedding gifts from that sunny day in late August 1950 – although nothing had been polished for years and a film of dust clung to the little spouts and delicate handles of the teapot and the gravy boat, the salt and pepper canisters, the sugar bowls and little trays for fish knives. On the mantelpiece, there were more photos of her sons and two vases with plastic snowdrops and a machine for making espresso coffee, which she got from someone in Saudi Arabia but which she had remained convinced was no more than an ornament. An enormous mound of old clothes was piled in the far corner. It was like a refuse heap in a charity shop, and it was impossible to get into that part of the room. Behind all the rags was a hi-fi black box record player, which had been my father's pride and joy when he was in the gramophone society in the 1950s. The members would meet in the Farnham Arms Hotel every fortnight and, at each meeting, a different member would play a selection of their favourite records while the others listened. I heard my father once say that he particularly enjoyed the evenings when the local doctor was in charge, because he loved opera and brought recordings of many famous arias, and he could bring *La Traviata* or *La Bohème* to life. The librarian was fond of music too and she would often tell me how wonderful the previous night's recital had been, describing the music in detail, while she stamped my copy of *Treasure Island* or *Kidnapped* when I went in for a new book after school. How anyone could describe a movement of classical music in terms of mountains, valleys and soft breezes astonished me, and her enthusiastic descriptions inspired me to take out my father's records sometimes from the shelves beneath the black box and listen to Gilbert and Sullivan or the piano music of Chopin.

On top of the black box there was a photo of Uncle

Oliver in a tuxedo, black overcoat and white scarf. It would have infuriated my father if he had seen Oliver smiling on top of his precious black box, but Father was long dead when the photo was put there, and by then Mother had forgotten what the black box was for. Oliver is beaming with joy in the photograph as he holds his arm around a young woman in an evening gown. He looks surprised and pleased at the camera, though he never married or spoke of any woman in romantic terms, which made it another strange memento by which to remember him.

Another television set had been placed in the corner of this room on a rickety wicker stool, so Mother could view it from the bed. Not that she needed high definition at that stage. She had lost interest in the material world. But I think she still needed images out there in the room to distract her from the things in her own mind. Two rolls of toilet paper and a bottle of air freshener sat on top of the television, within reach if she was sitting on the commode next to it.

Saint Bernadette viewed all this from a picture above the commode. It was a framed picture I had owned when I was a priest in Fermanagh, given to me by a woman who had been to Lourdes hoping to find relief from cancer or at least serenity on her deathbed.

In the centre of the room was a single bed, with a mattress which I had bought the same day as the chair. The electric blanket was off, but still plugged in. The sheets were crumpled, and the duvet was half rolled down. I pressed my hand into the pillow, making a dent, and then I could really imagine she had just moved the duvet away and got out of bed a few moments earlier. I suppose I should have sorted all this out when she first went into the nursing home, but I didn't.

On top of the little locker beside the bed there were various bottles of tablets, and empty Maalox bottles and an unopened naggin of brandy, and more handbags and a rosary of gaudy purple beads and a glass beaker that had once held Mother's teeth while she slept. There were prayer leaflets honouring saints, and memorial cards for various relations and friends, and three pictures of Padre Pio praying with his wounded hands joined before his face.

Inside the locker at the very back, behind more bed linen, my fingers found another rosary; old black beads with a gigantic crucifix which had been woven around my grandmother's fingers as she lay dying in a house on Bridge Street in 1963, and which my mother had cherished after that funeral.

I took the beads with me as I returned to the kitchen and placed them on the table beside the tin of chocolates. When I opened the round glass door of the washing machine, more nightdresses fell out on the floor, and I could see other small things inside which terrified me so I pushed them all back in and closed the door again.

Saucepans, pots and two frying pans sat on the small

87

cooker. And on the chair beneath the window, I noticed a red plastic basin, with a face towel draped on the side. There was a toothbrush, a tube of paste, a bar of soap sitting on a plastic dish in the basin. The Rayburn had once been fuelled by coal, and rarely went out and it was there that she used to cook chicken soup when I was a child, but in her seventies she had no one to cook for anymore, and the coal buckets were heavy, and what she ate herself she could heat in the microwave or boil on a small electric cooker in the back kitchen. But no smoke had risen in the Rayburn chimney for thirty years to disturb the crows that nested there. On top of the Rayburn, there was only a black kettle from my grandmother's world, a large packet of toilet rolls and half a dozen plastic bags with Dunnes Stores printed on them.

She saved bags each week when we went shopping because she hated paying the extra twenty-two cents for a new one. But we always forgot to bring a bag, and were obliged to buy one more each week. So the bags piled high on the Rayburn beside a blue plastic folder that contained the care workers' notes and log book. Every event that had happened in the house was written in there – what work had been done, what conversations or arguments had taken place, and what physical and emotional condition my mother had been in. It was a backup to contradict any false accusations that Mother might make about having been mistreated, robbed or neglected by the care worker.

I sat down on a hard chair at the table and took the black rosary beads in my hand and pressed them to my lips with a reverence that was more nostalgic than true. Like many other people in Ireland, I had outgrown the devotions of my childhood, the fervour that gathered us together in the shelter of a church. I suppose if I could have cried even then, it might have helped.

I'D BEEN DELIGHTED to find the sugar bowl in my studio. But it was also a warning. OK, she might be in Poland and it's only day one, but if I neglected the basic domestic chores now, what kind of condition would the place be in after six weeks? So I decided to make a better effort. I returned to the kitchen and made myself a breakfast from whatever scraps I could find. A kind of emptiness filled the little cottage. Shafts of light broke into the small room. I turned on a blow heater. To my surprise I found three eggs at the back of the empty fridge which

I boiled in a white enamel pot and I ate them all from the one cup, along with two slices of blue moulded bread I found in a press and which were edible enough once I cut out the mouldy bits and toasted them.

I wiped down the worktop mechanically, as I would do if the beloved were standing there beside me. It was the first moment that she surfaced in my mind. I could sense her hand on the dishes. I went into the bathroom and sensed her feet in the shower, and in the sun room I imagined I heard her talking about the loveliness of geraniums that she had taken in for the winter and the pot of aquilegia that she intended to plant out later in the spring. There were small buds coming now, but no one to notice them only me.

I had an urge to text.

Buds coming on that plant in the front room. Must water the aquilegia—

But halfway through the text, I desisted. She's wise and she had turned off her phone, and I ought to do the same. This was a time of separation, a time for each of us to withdraw, to forget the familiarity of each other's bodies, to stand untouched for a short while and listen to what was coming from inside. Then later we could embrace with love and joy, instead of just falling into each other's arms unconsciously because we wanted to find escape from interior weather.

So I made a list and I made a plan. The list was as extensive a catalogue as I could manage of what was needed in the house. Things like rashers, sausages, boxty, firelighters and so forth. I made the plan on a separate sheet, drawing a timetable, and then pencilling in what I might do from hour to hour.

I would get up at seven every morning and go for a walk in the mountains. Then I'd return and meditate. In the afternoons, I would read or write. And in the evenings, I would turn on the television, boil an egg and relax. It seemed to me like a perfectly swift path to enlightenment. When she returned home, I'd have half a book written, the place would be spotless, I'd be totally chilled out and the cat would have no hairballs. Everything was going to be perfect. And it was time to begin because already the sun was moving higher and the mountain beckoned.

I put on leggings and a big yellow raincoat and my sunglasses and a woollen hat, got into the jeep and drove farther up the mountain, beyond all the neighbours' houses until I passed a derelict council cottage by the bridge, where a couple had once raised six children. The house is now abandoned. The sight of derelict houses was never uncommon in Leitrim. The weather strips the plaster and the thatch and what remains in the forestry or at the end of a weedy lane is usually just the bare stones, the gable wall and the little holes where windows were long ago torn out by winter storms. But since the boom and subsequent collapse, there are many modern houses – semi-detached, urban dwellings – and many dainty little pebble-dashed cottages that the county council erected in the 1970s which are now empty. Some were never occupied. Some were shelter for poor rural families. And all will soon be rubble, tossed by diggers. The cottage by the bridge still had a slate roof intact. But the windows were boarded up. And the front door had been taken off its hinges so that the interior lay open to the elements. Sheep and sometimes horses take shelter there from the storms. I suppose houses don't look much different from any other stable to an animal.

I drove across streams and through forestry, until I came to a turn for the wind farm, a summit where once stood the entrances to mine shafts, and where local men went with lamps to dig out coal. They lay on their sides, stretched on the horizontal to scrape narrow seams, as the floor of the shaft filled with water. A community so oppressed that one miner was forced to dig a small shaft of his own from inside his bedroom down into the layers of clay and shale and coal beneath the house in order to keep his family warm. He brought up the fuel all winter without anyone knowing how he did it. The smoke rose from his chimney but he was never seen buying a single bag.

I drove as far as I could on the tarred road and then a mile farther on stones and rocks that fell away loose beneath the tyres of the jeep's huge wheels. And when I could make no more ground in the jeep, I stopped and walked on, clad in wet gear with a walking stick that a musician in Mullingar had given me years ago.

93

It's never easy to know what to wear on the mountain. When I wear leggings, an anorak, gloves and a woollen hat I think I look like Shackleton or Tom Crean, and then the sun comes out and I meet other hikers on the hills in their shirts and their jumpers slung around their waists and I feel like a pure eejit. But on the other hand, when the sky is blue, I sometimes leave the wet gear in the jeep and head up with just a walking stick and before I'm at the summit, a big nasty cloud of rain bursts out of nowhere and I'm drenched to the bone.

I always take the blackthorn stick. Not that I need it. It's just that men feel more secure when they're wielding a weapon. I think that's why bishops always have an elegant gold-plated shepherd's crook when they're processing down the aisle. And someone once told me that the word 'imbecile' denotes a man without a walking stick, which makes perfect sense to me. I remember a time when all the farmers in the pubs in Dowra would have a stick in one hand and a pint of Guinness in the other on a fair day. And there were men who would kill if someone took their personal stick. Mine is a blackthorn with the shinbone of a goat cut into the top as a handle. When I grasp it, I feel confident. It gives me courage. It enables me to feel like the musician, though the musician is more of a man than I am. He is certain in his masculinity. He is confident in his compassion. Maybe because, as a lover, he has a history of wildness. And there is nothing that becomes a man more than a good history. It makes his face pleasant and his heart satisfied, when he gets over forty. Sowing wild oats develops in a man some kind of tranquillity. His countenance exudes an ease that draws people to him.

As I walked up the steep incline, watching that my feet didn't slip on the scree and loose rock, the sun behind me rose into the fog, illuminating it from behind, so that it looked like a brilliant sheet covering the sky. And sometimes the fog blew away, leaving the hills clear and the windmills gleaming white in the sunlight. *Irish weather is the core of our melancholy*, I thought. The unpredictability of it. If it's raining, it's raining; if the sun is shining, the only question to ask is how long will it last. Not long. The fog comes again. Envelops us. No wonder half the country is depressed.

Below me I could see the rivers of Leitrim and Longford, the small lakes and the glorious Shannon, like thin steel threads, meandering around the drumlins. Closer to me on either side were hills. What we in Ireland defiantly refer to as mountains; highlands of bog, all brown and soggy for miles and miles around me and stretching as far as Sligo and the sea.

And up I went, still stumbling through the scree, until I reached a harder landscape where the bog lessened and heaps of grey shale stood twenty feet high on either side of the roadway, with boulders idle in the soft shale. This is a desert landscape. An Afghanistan of the mind where I could have imagined British troops coming around the bend, in armour-plated personnel carriers as they prepared to take out an enemy. This is not the quiet landscape of Yeats or Kavanagh. This is another Ireland. The hills up here were man-made with diggers or hand shovels centuries ago, by miners with the sweat of their brows. This is a landscape where men have made their mark. Even the townland names up here are personal, like Spion Kop, taken from a hill in South Africa where the British stood against the Boers and where men of the Connaught Rangers died in defence of an empire. And when that war was over, the men came home to Roscommon and Leitrim, and played in flute bands on Sunday afternoons, and worked the mines the rest of the week, and the name of the hill followed them like a shadow.

I walked through it all at a marching pace, with the musician's stick. Going uphill, trying to find in myself the kind of masculinity I see in the leisure centre, when the boys are lifting weights in the gym and their grunts carry all the way to the jacuzzi.

I was sweating and I was almost at the summit where various roads meander through small quarries of sand, resembling a desert landscape. There were markers posted to indicate the path to each turbine. The clouds at that point dispersed and I could see in the distance the grave of Queen Maeve on the top of Knocknarea and the head of Ben Bulben beneath which Yeats lies buried, and between the two mountains I could see Sligo bay. Closer to me was a broken turbine, its third blade lying down, limp, like the broken limb of a soldier.

I kept pushing at a brisk pace up the hills as my heart pumped furiously and my limbs ached but I felt joyful and happy. You can't beat a good walk for calming the mind. It might be lonely, but not even a room full of beautiful women in leotards doing yoga can induce the tranquillity that the sight of a wild hare on the crest of a hill has on my psyche.

The mountain walk was a great beginning to my retreat.

Of course I did try to reach enlightenment by stretching my yogic limbs in a room full of ladies in leotards with foam mats on a wooden floor and a glass wall and soft Zen music in the background. I was attending a privately run health centre on the outskirts of Mullingar. There was a series of large rooms with walls of glass looking out onto flower gardens, privately owned and rented to various holistic practitioners: yoga teachers, reiki masters, reflexologists and various adepts at massage in the Thai, Chinese and Brazilian styles who rented by the hour and charged their clients modest recession prices.

For the yoga class, we gathered on a Wednesday morning at eleven. The sun was pouring in through the window behind the teacher, who seemed like she was radiating light. I happened to be the only male present, apart from a sandalled, boyish journalist who had persuaded me to attend. After a short while, I found myself in contorted positions with my face always sideways or upside down or squashed on the floor and nearest to me was invariably a young woman in similar contortions, such that I found myself getting slightly aroused. At the coffee break, I explained that I feared I might have pulled a muscle and I retreated for ever from the intensity of group yoga classes. Although, on my way out, I passed another room where the door was open and a beautiful woman with dark skin and brown eyes wearing a white coat smiled at me.

'You're not from Mullingar,' I said.

'Brazil,' she replied, laughing.

She was standing at a bench that looked like an enormous ironing board except that there was a hole at one end.

I said, 'What's the hole for?'

She said, 'That is for your head.' And she described how a client would lie on the board with his or her face in the hole while Miss Brazil kneaded the muscles of the shoulders and lower back.

'What were you doing?' she asked.

'I was in the yoga class,' I confessed.

She roared laughing, and I knew immediately that in another life we could have been great friends.

But walking is a powerful yoga. And I love the mountain and the solitude of it and the freedom to talk aloud to myself since no one is listening except the sheep.

When I returned to the foothills and jeeped my way

back to the house, my chakras were open. At least they felt open. I mean if a policeman asked me where my chakras actually were, I wouldn't be able to tell him. But they felt open. And it was time now to meditate in earnest. I was ready for enlightenment.

MEDITATION IS NO joke. It's serious. It's a word that can be used to impress people. It implies that you're taking life seriously. You are grasping the essence of being. Sometimes on television chat shows, when celebrities are talking about their personal suffering or addiction or how they came to be the best guitarist or singer in the world, the interviewer will ask them what they do when they're not touring.

And sometimes they say, 'I meditate.'

Although I'm a bit uneasy with people who say they meditate and retain a completely straight face. Because in a way meditation is not something to do. It's not something you achieve. If you think you're meditating, then maybe you're not. If you think you're not, then maybe you are. As they say in Japan, if you name the bird then you cease to experience the song. So in naming the act of meditation you cease to meditate. Personally I just doze. I think dozing might be described as the Irish tradition of meditation. It's a space in your mind that opens out when you stay still. When you stop thinking. And your mind widens to take in everything at the same time and you're half aware of everything, as they say in Cavan. So that's what I would call meditation in the Cavan style.

Dozing.

Now and again, as the beloved and I are slurping our midday soup, she asks me a question.

'What are you going to do for the afternoon?'

I suppose it's a way of testing whether or not I'd like to join her in Lidl or Aldi, to follow her trolley around the aisles and share the fun of selecting which cheese we might eat next week. But I have only one reply.

'I'm going to meditate.'

Which means I'm going out to my studio, to light the stove and do nothing. Or rather, I'm going to resist doing anything. I'm going to take a break from everything. Because doing nothing is still doing something. So the wisdom is in the not doing. The complete non involvement in anything. Stillness. And if that's not a sure way to induce a beautiful doze then nothing is.

Irish people don't spend enough time dozing at the fire, gazing at the flickering flames in the stove or staring out the window at the birds on the peanut feeder. But I find that stillness grows in my body when I do these things and my mind becomes gentle. When nothing happens for the entire afternoon, it's lovely to just feel you are there. To be aware that you are there. It's what I used to be accused of doing in school. Back then it was called daydreaming. But today, as I pay attention to the flame in the stove, the flickering shadow, or the movement of a bird on a tree outside or the tiny shifting of the curtains with the wind I am not dreaming. I am awake in my lovely dozing. I feel like a baby in a cot with open eyes. I know I'm there. And I feel like an old man by the fire who knows that he has only a short while to live, and that the clock is ticking and each moment is precious.

'What are you doing in here?' the postman asked, one day he was obliged to come around to the studio behind the house with a parcel because he got no answer at the kitchen door.

'Nothing,' I said. 'I was just dozing.'

'There's no one in the house,' he said.

'Yes,' I said. 'I know.'

'Is she away?'

'She's in Poland,' I said.

'And is she coming back?' he wondered.

'Hard to tell,' I said. 'The future is a mystery.'

'That's true,' he agreed, as he stared out at the lake. 'We can never tell what's out there.'

I REMEMBER WHEN I lived in west Cavan in the 1970s, I used to finish work as a teacher at about four or sometimes three in the afternoon. I would drive up the hills from Blacklion and turn onto a small laneway that led to a remote farmhouse, where lived three young women in their late teens and their mother and father. I figured out that the best way to find girlfriends in those years was to befriend their mothers. I'd pop in unexpectedly and offer to fetch messages because I had a car, and I'd chat with the mother about anything from the weather to the price of lambs. When the girls arrived from work in the evening, I was already part of the family. In those days, courtship was a complex ritual in rural Ireland.

I would spend long afternoons sitting on the chair near to the range while the woman of the house mooched about preparing the evening meal. And then sometimes she'd sit down opposite me. We'd both be there on either side of the range, which would wheeze with heat. There was no Joe Duffy or talk shows or political debates on the radio to entertain us. Just the sound of rain. And when we had exhausted the possibilities of whether it might rain imminently or later in the evening or tomorrow morning or if, in fact, it was already raining, there wasn't much else to say. So the sitting continued. And both of us drifted into a different space, a timeless and beautiful womb of silence and presence. Each of us warmed the other and when I was going later she'd say, 'Thanks for calling,' as if I had done her a great service. And I too felt refreshed but at twenty-two years of age, I had no way of expressing how I felt to a middle-aged woman who had reared five children. The only thing we knew about Buddhism or Asian philosophy in those days was that a German woman who lived in a small cottage farther up the hill would pass the door sometimes with a great sack of groceries on her back. She had no car and locals would whisper to each other that she was one of those Hare Krishnas who came from Fermanagh, though nobody quite knew what exactly that meant.

The first time I went to a meditation session in the Buddhist Centre in Cavan, we got instruction on how to practise single-pointed concentration. They said to sit with a straight back, in a lotus or half-lotus or Zen position, and pick a spot at the end of the nose and, rather than close your eyes, focus on this spot and breathe in and out. Let the breath come and go as it pleases. Don't form it. Don't control it. Don't guide it. Allow the breath to come and go. As the thoughts come and go. And watch the breath. Watch the thoughts in the mind, rising and falling. But keep focused on the breath. In and out. With your eyes open and focused on some little spot at the end of your nose.

Of course, they meant a spot on the carpet in line with the end of the nose. I didn't get that. I thought they meant a spot that was actually on the end of my nose. So I was trying this for weeks, and going cross-eyed until I began to develop headaches every time I tried to do it. I think that's when I gave up on the formalities of Asian practice. At forty, my body was too unruly to be moulded into anything close to the thin whippet-like bodies of men and women in the group around me; men as supple as young ash plants and women as delicate as dithering ballerinas. I was out of my depth.

But over the years, I have definitely found a lot of spiritual consolation from sitting at the stove and doing nothing and it's great after all these years to discover that I was actually meditating without realising it.

On this occasion, of course, it was going to be different. I was going to do it right. And so I began. Hoping that the walk had emptied my mind. Hoping to focus on my breath.

I took out a little meditation cushion. I lit a candle at the far end of the room. I found a small Buddha statue in a drawer and set him up on the table. I sat on the cushion and waited. Sadly, no great realisation or sense of enlightenment surfaced. In fact, I couldn't keep my mind still for two consecutive seconds. The elephant was all over the place. For example, I started looking at the flame, but began thinking of a dinner party. I chastised myself. *I must discipline this elephant*, I told myself. But for some reason, I connected the image of an elephant with a badger. I know they're not the same size but they do wobble in a similar fashion when they're trotting.

And that led me to think about the real badger. He's invisible to me because he only moves around at night. But when we came here twenty years ago, I found his track through the garden, like a human pathway. He came over the ditch and into our sloping field and down at a diagonal towards the road on the southside of the property. Back then, the place was a soft hill, curved and smooth, and beneath the grass there was a million tons of shale.

In time, Sean Quinn arrived, and he walked the land and pointed to where the sandstone ledge ended and where the shale had collected millions of years earlier, creating the hill that our house now sat on. Sean desperately wanted that shale and before long he had secured a deal with farmers around us to dig out a quarry just on the edge of our property. The diggers came and dug for months, and then years, until the hill vanished, except the ledge our house was on, and, at the end of our garden, a cliff emerged, dropping sixty feet down into a pond below. It was a dramatic change to the landscape. We had bought a house on a hill and it became a house on the edge of a cliff. Instead of having a few ditches as a view, we had the entire length of Leitrim in our windows, and mountains stretching from the top of Lough Allen to the southern point near Drumshanbo.

But the badger wasn't pleased. The warrens beneath the ground that had probably been there for decades or even centuries must have endured a terrible onslaught from the JCBs over the course of ten years. Then the recession came, and Sean Quinn was destroyed and the quarry closed and the gates rusted and heather grew around the pond below us as we looked down over the cliff.

When I'd come back from the walk, I'd gone down to the end of the garden to examine the ash tree. It used to flower every summer and then produce a glorious flush of red berries. But gradually it had become choked with ivy, and when new fences were being put down by the quarry people, the tree was in the way so they cut it to a stump. However, in the intervening years, the roots had sent out new shoots and now a new daughter tree stood beautifully bare, beside the old stump and against the backdrop of the lake. I didn't hug it, but I certainly curled the flat of my two hands around the bark of the young sapling and offered her a few words of encouragement. And that's when I saw the badger track. The pathway had reappeared, exactly as it had been twenty years ago, a zigzag line through the long grass, the heather, the rushes and even through the fence. Mr Badger or his grandchildren now moved across the earth on the same lines as they had done for generations, long before the upheavals that had befallen them during the time of the boom and the diggers in Mr Quinn's quarry.

It took a lot of effort to get the badgers out of my mind and to start focusing on my breath again, but the next thing that distracted me was the banjo, because I couldn't ignore it in the corner of my eye. It had been lying neglected in its case beside the computer desk for months. I don't play the banjo. But the musician in Mullingar who gave me the walking stick also gave me the banjo for my sixtieth birthday.

Perhaps I ought to have taken it up and played something. I could pluck out 'Amazing Grace' and the 'Leitrim Jig'. I could play three chords – G, D and C – which I'd downloaded onto my iPhone the day after my birthday, so I wanted to quench the candle and pick up the instrument. I guessed that most people would find strumming a musical instrument far more soothing for the mind than trying to focus on a spot at the end of their nose. My nose as it happened.

But I decided to persevere. I banished the banjo and began to focus once again on my breath. Breathing in and breathing out. I took a quick glance at the little plastic clock on the bookcase. I had begun at 11 a.m. and figured it might now be near midday, and I wanted to get a Scollan's lunch before 1 p.m. because all the school students come then and create a bottleneck queue for lasagne. But the clock said it was only 11.10.

The reason why my guru once told me that the mind is like an elephant was to explain how very hard it is to discipline the mind. Even with strong ropes, it's not very easy to keep an elephant still. It will go where it wants unless it is trained. But beginning again to think of the mind as an elephant was making me tense. *I can't win here*, I told myself. If my mind was a horse, I wouldn't be able to control it. An elephant is way beyond me. It's ridiculous. Why bother at all?

I was now fighting myself. It's a terrible twist that I get into sometimes when I'm trying to meditate. I'm sitting there as still as a statue of the Buddha but inside it's mad. It's a war zone of rage. I'm flitting through all the people I loathe. All the reasons I should loathe myself. It's like a therapy group in my head but everyone has gone berserk and is talking at the same time. I end up more stressed out than when I first began. And though I was still sitting on the cushion, my hands joined in my lap and my eyes to the ground, I was contorted in fury, and full of frustrated desires to scream or kick the cat or just shoot someone.

And maybe that's why my mind eventually drifted to Afghanistan again. Or maybe it was because of the documentary that had surfaced in my BBC podcasts the previous day as I was driving home.

A soldier had been talking about his tour of Helmand province.

'We were driving over a ridge,' he'd said, 'and we came under fire. There were Taliban trenches all around us, which the Taliban had left half an hour earlier, and now we were in them and they were firing at us.'

He'd said he liked techno music and that when he was preparing for a tour of duty he made playlists for his iPod. He used dance music for physical exercising and country and western music to put him to sleep at night when he was lying in some half-dug grave under the Afghan sky, but when he was in battle, he found techno music was by far the best soundtrack for killing. And he described what it was like on one occasion to be in battle, shooting away at other people.

'They started shelling us with rockets,' he'd said. 'We were fighting them non-stop for forty-eight hours. And in those situations, if you get something wrong, you're going to die. And as you're picking your target, and as you squeeze the trigger and watch the target fall, you must be focused. And when you see the target fall down, you flick a map to give grid references to the guy on top even though the bullets are still flying over your head. But there is no fear because you are busy and focused. The fear only rises when someone shouts "Stores!" and you know that the aircraft who got your co-ordinates has just dropped its load and it's on its way down and you feel sickly for a moment because if you got it wrong, it will land on you. And then it detonates. Your heart leaps. And you're back up firing again. And of course you're fully focused.'

'Now that,' I'd said to myself, 'is what I call a man.' And I'd been impressed by how much music meant to him. I could just imagine them all with their iPods and mp3 players banging away intensely and finding more focused concentration in those moments than I would ever find in twenty years of looking at a spot at the end of my nose.

Earphones gave him the illusion of privacy when he needed to relieve himself sexually in the middle of battle, he'd explained – but I didn't quite understand what he meant.

'And just as in sex, when the killing stopped, the elation was intense,' he'd said. 'A euphoric release. But empty.'

That's what he'd said. The man was having some kind of mental orgasm as he killed other people. And he was euphoric about it. And then empty. You just can't beat the BBC.

'I had a metallic taste in the mouth like after adrenaline,' he'd said, 'but empty.' And he'd grown accustomed to it. And he'd needed more each time. More risk. It's what turns men into boys. I could just imagine a squad of them with headphones and sexy battle fatigues, like warrior princes going off to slaughter, and them creating playlists for the action on their little iPods.

'And when you're fighting,' he'd said, 'when you're scrapping all the time during an engagement, when it has become just an old-fashioned shooting match, it's just like trying to get through a crowd to get water at the bar during a dance. So there's a bias towards dance music. I mean it makes sense.'

Right. Of course. Techno music, for the war on terror. You learn something new every day.

'Bullets flying and the sound of RPGs is music in itself,' he'd declared. 'Sometimes I would put on my cans and listen to Josh Wink as all hell was breaking loose. Oh, yes, definitely,' he'd concluded, 'it focuses the mind.'

Well, why the fuck was I wasting my time staring at the floor when I couldn't focus at all? I was up on my feet in an instant and quenched the candle in complete frustration and went outside and paced up and down the garden, using the musician's walking stick to whack last year's nettles and me in a rage that I couldn't quite understand.

If she hadn't been in Poland at that moment, what would I have done? If she were near me, if she were in the kitchen, what would I do? I would have gone into the house for a cup of tea, a slice of currant bread or a bowl of chilli soup; whatever was going. It would have calmed me down. Or if she had been in her studio at the end of the garden, I could have gone down and sat by her stove as she sculpted some new figure in clay. If she were not in Poland, she might have sustained me. Any kind of small talk would have taken me away from the badger and the soldier and the war in Afghanistan, because as sure as there is shite in a goose, meditation wasn't helping me.

MY MOTHER WAS afflicted with loneliness. I suppose it eats away at everyone eventually. Of course, it's glaringly obvious in the old bachelors from up the hills buying their bread and rashers in village supermarkets, and you can't miss it in widowers who take up carpentry just to belong to a club, or widows who go to yoga classes. And there's often someone in the local book club or drama group who has had a sudden bereavement and is trying to get out of the house. And they walk with such a heavy weight that their loneliness is easy to feel. But there are lonely people in marriages, too. Unnoticed. Those whose smiles are a prison because they just can't admit even to themselves that their partner is a waste of space, in case it brings the world tumbling down on their children's heads or in case their mothers would say, 'I told you so.'

Sometimes when I see a couple sitting together in the corner of a bar, I can't avoid noticing how she glows in his presence, smiling like the sun, holding her face close to his, but when she slips away to the bathroom, the smile evaporates and her expression is drained and uneasy – and then does the make-up seem just a touch overdone. And all her gloss and powder seem like a prison door behind which she too might be wondering why she always feels alone. Maybe everyone is lonely and maybe it's incurable. And no matter how many relations hold hands around a deathbed, there is no escaping the solitude of that final letting go. And maybe that's the secret of this universe. Certainly when I look at the happy young woman my mother was in pictures from the past, she didn't know what the universe had in store for her.

Her face blazed with happiness as she walked the streets of Cork, arm in arm with her friends. And even when we were growing up, she loved having people come to stay, and preparing dinners, and wheeling trollies of freshly made buns into the drawing room when the room was full, and making chicken soup dinners when her children came home from university for a weekend, and bringing buns to the old women in the annex of the county home on Sunday afternoons, and playing golf, and going to visit her sisters in Westmeath and Dublin, and staying up all night in our house at parties when there were other people there who would listen to her stories – and all that time she loved other people. She needed other people. But like all young people, she never thought she'd get old. Like many old people, she didn't know why her heart had grown melancholic. I suppose the heart is the core of the problem. She reached out all her life to be held by others, because we all need to be held by something or someone. And as she got older, that holding was less firm, and the friends dwindled until they were few and far between, and she realised that loneliness is what kills us all in the end.

She was in her seventies when the beloved and I first moved to Leitrim. That was in 1993. She drove herself to our front door on the first Christmas we were in the house, and again at the end of January, for our daughter's first birthday party. But two years later, she was going downhill. She was seventy-nine and we thought she wouldn't last much longer. She stopped driving. She was short of breath. And she had dwindled into a small bird of a woman in a tweed suit. She sat in the kitchen of our little cottage in the hills above Lough Allen on Christmas morning. Myself and my beloved went for a walk around noon, as the turkey roasted slowly in the oven. Outside it was snowing and the world was silent and white.

'I'd prefer to watch mass on the television,' Mother had said.

So off we went, me and the beloved, arm in arm, while the old woman held herself in rigid attention for the pope, and the child slept in the cot in the front room.

I thought it might have cheered my mother to be alone with her grandchild, but it didn't. She was still watching the pope when we returned.

'How was the child?' I'd asked.

'No trouble,' she'd replied, as if the baby might have been a sheep.

But now I know that while we were out walking, she was writing in her diary – a tiny book, hardly bigger than a cigarette box, with just one line for each day of the year.

Christmas Morning. Last night they had visitors in the front room. A young couple. Teachers. I sat in the kitchen all night at the television. Very lonely. No wireless.

Later that night, alone in her bedroom, she wrote about Christmas Day.

My pudding and cake went down well, I think.

On Stephen's Day, she wrote again.

Not feeling well. I want to go home.

She stayed another six days but insisted on going home before New Year's Day. We watched her pack her bag like a sorrowful child heading off to a grim boarding school on the last day of December, and we put the small presents we had given her on Christmas morning into the boot of the car. On each of the six days, unbeknownst to us, she had written another terse report in her diary.

Not well today.

We had dinner in Ballinamore on the way to Cavan and when we got to her house, I discovered a leak from a pipe in the bathroom. The ceiling was ruined. I phoned a man, who promised to come out the following day and fix it. I kissed her on her dry, powdery cheek at the front door and drove away.

'Ring me when you get home,' she said.

I tried her number later in the evening, but she didn't answer. I left a message wishing her a happy new year and guessed she had gone to bed early.

In her diary she wrote.

Very upset about the water. He did nothing. I have no one to help me.

And the next day.

Stayed up to watch the New Year on television. Nobody rang.

And the next day.

Nobody called. Bad day.

She lived through sixteen more Christmases, mostly spending them with us, either in Leitrim or Mullingar, and they were always much the same. There was a glass wall between mother and son. We went through various rituals and we sometimes brushed our cheeks against each other when we met or parted, but that was about it. Intimacy was a project we had both abandoned.

When she came for Christmas, we tried to do as much as we could for her. We warmed the bed. We put on big fires in the front room. We got water for her at night and a bedside lamp that she could manipulate with ease if she needed to go to the toilet. But nothing worked.

She was isolated in a little world of her own, which she tracked in her diary but was resolute in keeping from her son. And she teared up with automatic melancholy when other folk walked into her presence. I asked her once why she didn't share more with me. She said, 'I don't want to be upsetting you.'

But she did upset me. She was unhappy all the time, and that made me sad.

Sometimes, I wondered why. Did I not visit her often enough? Did she feel she ought to be living with us even though we only had a cottage with two tiny bedrooms? And no matter how many Sundays we took her to dinner in the

Kilmore Hotel, or no matter how many times we brought her to family festivals, birthday parties, or for Christmas, we never really were able to cross the line and reach the space where she lay wounded for so many years. In hotels, she always insisted on paying for the dinner. At Christmas, she brought puddings, Christmas cake and bottles of whiskey. But when Christmas or Easter or the child's birthday was over, she went home to her own house and closed the door, and wrote in her diary and said nothing more to us.

I would often spend half an hour on the phone.

'What's wrong, Mammy?' I would say. And she would break into willowy sobs.

'Nothing,' she would reply. 'Nothing at all.' The silence would stretch out between us on the line like a great empty beach in Donegal and we might as well have been at either end of that beach, whispering into the wind.

'Please tell me what's wrong, Mammy. Did I do something to annoy you?' Over and over again. Until eventually she would say it again: 'Nothing.' And the phone would go dead, leaving me full of anxiety that I had failed as a son.

Maybe she didn't have the language to express her terror of old age or her rage at ending up so frail. Perhaps there was something about growing old that she couldn't accept or articulate.

And yet with other people, she could be the direct opposite. When other people held her, called her, touched her, she responded like a little girl who is admired in a new dress. This was the most important mystery about her life – that, alone, she sank deep into the dark and yet when she was teased into company, she became almost alarmingly jolly. She was vivacious. And she was even jolly in old age when anyone reached out to her. When her neighbours came to the door with the newspapers or groceries or collecting for the parish, she'd bring them into the drawing room and show them pictures of her grandchild and talk about how well her children were doing in the world and gossip for hours about other neighbours. She wouldn't let them go for hours, because she needed them so much.

And yet if, subsequently, I phoned her and enquired if she had seen anyone over the previous few days, she would leave a pause on the line that had a kind of anger in it, and eventually she would whisper, 'Nobody.'

THE SAME NOBODY I was left with when the beloved was in Poland. And I feared that the days would pass slowly and that I would be bored with no one to talk to. But I was wrong. In fact, the days flew.

It snowed twice. Rainstorms battered the roof at night, and the gutters got clogged with pine needles blown from the trees and the water began to overspill from the guttering onto the window sills. One night, the electricity went out and I sat by the fire reading from a Kindle, and I lit the stove in the sun room and then fried potato cakes, eggs and rashers in a pan on top of the stove. It felt like camping out.

Every morning, I made a bowl of porridge and a pot of coffee. I went to the studio and lit the stove there. I sat looking out at the mountain. Around noon, I went walking up the hill. In the afternoons, I sat again in the studio, dozing, eating apples and drinking coffee. On the first day, I had made a shrine by clearing a small table and layering it with blue Mongolian prayer scarves and white Tibetan prayer scarves and I brought out a statue of Buddha from the glass case. A precious Buddha statue I had got from the reincarnation of the King of Tibet in India years before. I had put a candle beside it. I wanted to set out the water bowls as well, but when I saw them in the drawer corroded from having been left unused for too long, I'd decided to leave them where they were.

After five days alone, I had seen nobody apart from the postman, whom I saw occasionally through the window as he dropped electricity bills and flyers for Aldi in the letterbox or when he knocked on the glass door of my studio with a parcel. I had planned to clean the house to a standard of military perfection because I've always had the notion that with one person away, cleaning would require less effort. But after almost a week, things were getting more chaotic.

The dirty clothes defeated me. I put on a wash, probably on too high a heat, which turned the bed sheets pink because I had thrown in some particularly red tartan pyjama bottoms, which I had been given the previous Christmas to match the pair of tartan slippers. I wasn't bothered about that, apart from being angry with the pyjamas. First, they killed my libido and now they were destroying the sheets. I dragged them out of the tumbler and hissed at them as if I was holding a disobedient dog.

'You fucking stupid excuse for pyjamas,' I said.

I do know that pyjama bottoms are an inanimate object and incapable of feeling. I know they didn't worm their way into the washing machine unbeknownst to me. But being alone has many strange effects on the mind, and I had begun to develop a compulsion to vent my anger at the most innocuous of objects around me.

Drying clothes was another difficulty. I couldn't master the art of drying anything outside. I presume it's possible because the beloved does it all the time. But women may have some secret ability to sense when the rain is going to stop, so they can dash out and throw everything on the line immediately and take them in again two hours later before the rain resumes.

I decided to dry them in the house. I even found three clotheshorses in the shed that had been there since the time the child was in Baby-gros, and I set them up in the sun room and lit the stove. We have central heating, but we also have four stoves – one for her studio, one for my studio, one for the office and one for the sun room. They were bought one at a time, and the theory was that they saved money. But the stove in the sun room is rarely used, and so it smoked all day while I was out in my studio chanting like a Mongolian Lama. Even the cobwebs went sooty. I had no alternative but to put on the central heating and leave the clotheshorses stacked against the radiators all night. But that didn't work either. Maybe I stacked up too much because the radiators just warmed the wet garments and detergent filled the room with a soft damp aroma in the morning.

After that, I didn't bother with clothes. I put the wet ones back in the machine, given that many of them were sooty from the smoking stove, and I resolved not to bother changing the clothes I was wearing for the rest of the month. I just needed to be careful. After that, I allowed my elephant go where he wanted. I was going to suit myself. Let the elephant do what he likes and sit where he wants and wear pyjamas. Don't keep trying to improve him. Besides, no one was going to know if I didn't change my clothes for the month.

That attitude clearly suited me. I relaxed. I started to become gentle with myself. I stopped pushing myself out of bed in the mornings or pushing myself up the hill for exercise or pushing myself into the kitchen to tidy up. *Just leave things as they are*, I thought. 'Let the universe

125

unfold, man,' as my artistic friends say when they're rolling a doobie. 'Give the poor fucken elephant a break.'

Yes, my libido had gradually been declining since I began wearing tartan pyjamas but now even my need for other people was fading. My interest in the postman or the radio was dying. I was drifting into a soft, unfocused coma.

My only stimulation came from the wilderness. The majestic Lough Allen and Sliabh an Iarainn, the Scots pines with their long hanging branches over the door, the storms at night and the magpie that struggled to grip the moving branch and save himself from the sleet and snow. He was marching about on the water tank one morning for so long that I felt he had things to tell me. I think the beloved used to feed him bits of bread, so he was probably missing her. And he had the courage to hop towards me across the water tank until he was quite close; one eye staring at me like my friend the General in bad humour. I could actually imagine him speaking as I covered the ash bucket with a plastic bag.

'Where's that woman gone?' I imagined him saying.

'None of your business.'

'She was nice.'

'It's none of your business,' I repeated out loud.

'It will be,' he said, 'if you're running the show much longer. Jesus, look at this place.'

He stared at me and then at the ash buckets.

True enough, we had four buckets for ashes but they were all full and the wind was blowing ash everywhere.

'This place is in shit,' the magpie declared.

'Fuck off,' I said. 'Go find your own breakfast.'

I was trying to get the ashes from the bucket into the plastic bag and he was so aggressive that I got distracted.

It's a tricky operation. You have to cover the entire bucket with the bag, then turn the bucket upside down so that the ashes fall cleanly into the bag and then you make sure not to take the bucket out too soon in case the ash dust blows all over the yard.

I executed everything very well, except for one part – you're not supposed to do it with last night's ashes in case they're still hot.

'For fuck's sake,' I screamed as the black plastic melted and the ashes fell in a formless lump like loose snow.

'Heh-heh-heh-heh-heh,' the magpie cackled, so I took a stone and flung it at him. But I missed. Although I did hit the postman, who was coming around the gable of the house. I laughed it off and accepted the mail; a brochure from Sky and *The Path to Freedom*, a dissertation on an ancient Tibetan text by the Dalai Lama which I had ordered from Amazon in a flush of optimism when my beloved first announced she was going to Poland.

'Them magpies are whores,' I declared to the postman, affecting the tone of tribes indigenous to the Cavan region. 'If I had a fucken gun I'd scatter the lot of them,' I added, which I suppose just shows how much I needed to read something by the Dalai Lama.

Clearly meditation wasn't doing me any good.

I considered the situation when the postman had clipped the door of his van closed, smiled at me through the window and driven off up the hill. It was too late in the day to be trying to communicate with gods or gurus, I thought, and I decided to dismantle my shrine and put away the statue of the Buddha. To coin a phrase – you can't teach an old elephant new tricks.

I suppose that was a fundamental act of despair. The truth is that the future always offers limitless possibilities. We can never predict what will happen next. For example, the beloved might never return from Poland. Who was to say? Maybe she would find someone else out there on the side of the road and fall in love over a few vodkas, or succumb to the power of prayer and turn herself in at the door of a monastery in some remote and snowy mountain from where she would never emerge and I would never find her. I might be traipsing across the Tatra Mountains for the remaining years of my life calling her name. There was no point in being anxious about the future, because the future is unknown. All I could do was try to survive for a while without her.

I know that sitting still for half an hour a day, and

128

avoiding television and Facebook and looking into the lake, can have a great calming effect on lots of other people. I've seen them chilled out sometimes at Buddhist retreats, like they've been stiffened by the faintest lair of shellac sprayed on their skin as they sit immobile in the lotus position for hours. But my fists were clenched, I was frightening the magpies, the postman may have suspected I was having a nervous breakdown, and the house was a kip.

So I abandoned everything. I abandoned the Buddha and the prayer shawls and the candles and the incense and all the books and leaflets and pictures of dakinis. I put them all in a drawer and I sat by the stove in the empty room for a while, saying, 'Just take it easy and be gentle with yourself.' Over and over again I said it. 'Let the old elephant go where he wants.'

I was watching the rhythm of the flames behind the glass door. If there was an elephant in the room, then he was standing completely still, and tranquil, like he was made of gossamer and filled with light and he was about to fly off over the lake.

'Maybe I'm already enlightened,' I whispered, with not another soul present, unless you consider the millions of other Buddha beings, bodhisattvas and the communion of Catholic saints, Doctor Who and Jesus and Mary, and really so many more that I can't go through them all. I believe in them all. I couldn't see them but I felt they were surrounding me, like a swarm of bees, and I decided to address them formally in this crucial moment.

'I apologise for being angry with the magpie and the pyjama bottoms,' I said. 'After all, what harm have they done me? And I'm sorry I was fretting about cleaning the house. I realise none of it matters.'

And in that single instant, I felt enlightened in the way that ordinary folk are enlightened. Just like the widow woman in west Cavan who used to say the rosary in the church on quiet afternoons, and then slap herself with holy water and walk on down to the shop to make lewd jokes with the other women about the young curate. Just like the old philosopher in Clare Island who made his own whiskey and had a handlebar moustache and philosophised by his own fireside for eighty winters. And all the women with headscarves who used to sit in the shelter shed in Lough Derg through the night talking about the quality of soda bread in the midlands. And the shepherd in Lizzy Buggy's Bar in Dowra, whose dog was always under the legs of his high stool and who used to sit with one glass of stout all afternoon, listening to the clock, and looking out the window at the children coming from school and seeing in them the same beautiful innocence that he regarded every spring in newborn lambs.

Maybe enlightenment is nothing more than a highly developed emotional intelligence, or what used to be described as common sense; a word that long ago faded from the lexicon of mental health.

And then the good feeling vanished, like the vicarious sunlight in Leitrim that often withers behind a sudden cloud. I no longer felt enlightened and the only thing I wanted was to go into Tesco. I had an intense craving for everything. Every lust and appetite that had been sleeping in me woke up at the same moment. I was so consumed by my general appetites that I was almost afraid to get into the jeep in case I'd crash. But Jesus, Mary and Saint Joseph, I fucking needed Tesco. I wanted Tesco. I wasn't going to cling to the dry solitude of meditation if I didn't feel like it. I wasn't going to clench my fist all day in some act of resistance and say, 'I must not submit to my appetites, because I'm on a journey of spiritual inquiry.' Fuck that. Let it go. Stop clinging to spiritual inquiries. I was off to Tesco.

And it was glorious. So many people with shopping trollies, so much colour and light and the decadent excess of glossy products on the shelves. And I was dizzy at the sight of women again. Buying too much and bringing it all home. The lady on the till asked me if I had a clubcard.

'A what?'

'Do you have a clubcard?'

'Ah, listen,' I said. 'Do I look like I have a clubcard?'

'No,' she said, looking at me and laughing, 'you don't.'

And her good humour encouraged me to continue, not quite knowing what I was talking about.

'Sure, in the long run none of us have clubcards,' I said.

'You're dead right,' she said.

'If we only had the clubcards,' I said, 'we'd be singing.'

She laughed again.

Not that I understood what she was laughing at either, or what a clubcard was, but I had just had so much fun meandering up and down the aisles after being two weeks on my own that I was enormously over-excited.

And I got so much stuff I didn't need, and then came home and cooked a curry and ate it with rice as I sat at the television watching *Girls*.

The cat was looking at me and whining as I ate. It was a devastating moment. I had not thought about her in Tesco. I had thought only of myself. And here she was like the reincarnation of some great teacher in a former lifetime, chastising me. She and I may have been together for endless lifetimes. She may have been my mother in a former life or I hers. She, I believe, was certainly my precious guru at some stage and now it was my responsibility to mind her. So I told her that, in the morning, I would go to the vet and get her a bag of Science Plan, her favourite dish. I apologised and said that, for now, I could only offer her some curry. I put a little curry and rice on her saucer. She turned her nose up once or twice, but eventually she dug in with such enthusiasm for the hot spices that I felt it was almost a confirmation that she was indeed my precious teacher in a former life

132

at the Metropole Hotel. In every picture, she laughs openly, her smile so loving and joyful that I am forced to ask if this is the same face that I saw on the pillow the night she died.

I held a letter in my hand that was written in India by a nun, who had heard the news of her engagement in June 1950. Maureen, a childhood friend, had joined the Loreto convent and was sent to Calcutta from where she wrote to Mother wishing her 'every joy and happiness in your new life'.

The letter goes on:

> I'm longing to hear everything about yourself and your future husband. I wish I knew the date of your wedding so that I could be united with you in prayer on that morning.

The nun was teaching in a school, beginning her classes at 7 a.m., and sleeping on the roof of the building with the other sisters at night because of the heat. And now she was writing in blue ink, and underlining words for emphasis. I held the letter in my hands, wishing my mother had shown it to me at some stage, even in old age, and said, 'Look at this!', and we could have laughed and cried at the brevity of a human life. Instead, she had folded it neatly away and placed it with three photographs of the nun at the back of a drawer in her dressing table, where it rested for over fifty years until I held it in my hands on the day of her burial.

I noticed an electric razor in the bathroom that my father

had used when he was old. It was on a shelf under the sink. Something intimate about him still remained on the teeth of the little Ronson machine, and it occurred to me that he might have been the cause of her sorrow. Perhaps, in private, he had been a monster to her. He might not have enjoyed sex. The union might have been arranged. Her expectations might have been based on too many romantic films seen with her friends in Cork. Or perhaps, at thirty-four, she had discovered too late that a forty-eight-year-old man could be a cold authoritarian fish in the starchy world of the Irish middle classes in 1950.

I was desperate to know what had wounded this beautiful woman. I was speculating wildly until I found other pictures of the young couple together that proved me wrong. It was as if the house was talking back to me, telling me that there was a different story for me to uncover. I found heaps more photographs in her purses, in drawers, in wardrobes and under her bed and in a shoe box and out in the coal shed in a Jacob's biscuit tin. I found albums of her wedding and maps of County Kerry from her honeymoon, and postcards I had sent to her from Italy in 1985, and postcards she had sent from Donegal on that same honeymoon in 1950, and pictures of her children in the 1960s, and letters from friends on the birth of her boys and pictures of her with himself in different parts of Ireland and pictures of her as an old woman in Belgium and Finland and Saudi Arabia when she went off with groups of other old people on adventures that I had long forgotten about. I found her laughing with my brother in Newfoundland and on her own at the end of a pier in Sweden. I found pictures of myself and of her one single grandchild everywhere. And I found cookbooks and recipes and stacks of magazines with knitting patterns. And letters.

The house was singing to me. It was giving up its secrets. It was happy. It was saying, 'Look here and there and here again, you'll find evidence of her love that you had forgotten about.' I found a letter I had written to her when I was ten. It fell out of a high-heeled shoe under the stairs. It was from Donegal saying how much I missed home and how I hoped she was feeding the cat.

'Look in the attic too,' some voice whispered in my head. 'For there are old suitcases up there and they are stuffed with hats and further treasures.'

She looked happy standing outside the church on her wedding morning or kneeling at the altar rails with the white veil still around her flowery hat. Leaning on her mother at the hotel door later on, and among her sisters around the breakfast table. Lined up with her brothers on the street. She looked happy two months later at the County Council Annual Dinner Dance in the town hall. On that occasion, she wore a white evening gown, immaculately folded around her waist and falling to her ankles. She wore her wedding and engagement rings and a gold watch on her wrist that he had bought her the previous year. And she wore a locket, with pictures of him and her inside. I know they are inside because I was holding the locket in my hand as I looked at the photograph. I held the rings and the watch and I scrutinised her smile and her white evening dress in the photograph. It had a high collar and a huge rose clipped on the right lapel. He sat beside her, intense as a young scholar, wearing a dinner jacket. The shirt, waistcoat and dickie-bow were white. On his lapel there was a round badge that said 'Committee'. And I held the faded badge too in my hand, as I gazed at that photograph.

All these things she had kept hidden. All these moments she had kept secret. Cherished or buried, I don't know. She never showed them to us. She never had them framed. They just gathered dust. And then she died. And then, only then, could I hold them.

She was eighty in 1996, but she spent over another decade refusing to answer the phone and scribbling useless things on tiny pages and casting notes into drawers, or behind the television set, or tossing them under the bed or lodging them at the back of wardrobes. I found evidence of every argument she had ever had with the ESB or the social welfare office or the county council about her pension or a car dealer with whom she had an altercation about repairs to her Ford Escort – all recorded in small pages torn from notebooks and tidied away into envelopes in the back of a drawer where she had kept her chequebooks. I found four one-line cuttings from the *Anglo-Celt*. One was her marriage notice. Two were notices of the births of her children. And the final one was her husband's death notice. Each one was terse and to the point and they were pasted into the inside sleeve of her prayer book.

I found her diary for 1995, as small as a cigarette box with one line available for every day of the year.

After writing a few terse notes about Christmas that year, which she had spent with us in Leitrim, the entries in the diary continue in the same melancholic despair through the new year.

No water in the house.

Went to doctor today.

Waiting for hours.

Lunch in hotel. No respect.

Raining. Fed up.

Can't find camera.

Terrible day.

Terrible lonely.

No one called.

On the story goes, all through January as she endured the snow and frost, confined to the house, afraid to walk the steps up to the cathedral for fear of slipping, and marking in her diary only pain and the price of food. The pittance she spent on her weekly groceries – six rashers, the local newspaper, a pint of milk, sticks for the fire, a bail of turf briquettes, a tin of soup. And at the end of the month, she recorded an important date: 27 January. 'Celebrated birthday today,' she writes. 'Bought three buns.'

It was her eightieth year. Another year measured out in her diary by the random litany of needs – teabags, bones for soup, barley mix, firelighters, sliced pans, tapioca, celery, cheese, lemons and pyjamas and yoghurt and slices of Brady's ham. And she had plenty of time to measure and record – on all those long endless Sundays that she spent alone in bed, when she wouldn't answer the phone – her difficulties in the toilet, her stomach bugs, her little bowl for porridge waiting idle in the microwave that she was too sick to reach. Her slippers. The clips for her hair that she had used fifty years earlier when she'd been going out to that first County Council Annual Dinner Dance. And the diaries. Those terse notes, like enigmatic clues to her heart. And the envelopes with groceries listed on the back. The delicate fabric of her reduced circumstance, all the fragments that made up a spatial memorial to an entire life held there like dust in the shafts of sunlight. It was like walking into a museum of her unconscious mind.

I touched her things but I could not touch her. I touched the armchairs her husband had bought for their first home, two rented rooms on the first floor of the Commercial

140

Hotel, and the bookcase where he had stored his books and where she had stored all the memories of his life when he died. I held in my hands a delph chamber pot that I remember my father using in his later years. When I was a child, I would see him running along the corridor in the mornings on white spindly legs, in his pyjama top.

I held Mother's beautiful clothes gathered over six decades. I touched the mohair cardigans, the tweed suits and jackets, the woollen slacks and silk blouses. Everything neatly folded, I opened, hugged and replaced. I examined the skirts and then hung them back again in the wardrobes where she had arranged them as if she might use them tomorrow. As if the last time she had put anything away, she had put it away with the hope of taking it out later to dance again. The small hats, the berets in green, brown, black, cream and rusty orange, stacked neatly on the corner of a shelf. The five flowery umbrellas under the hall table. The volumes of *Woman's Way* piled under the stairs with knitting patterns 'for lace dresses you can wear on the beach' and recipes written in her own hand for how to cook a trout.

Switch on the oven. Put on potatoes. Grease three tins. Melt the margarine. Prepare the stuffing for fish and tomatoes. Remove rind from rashers. Wipe fish, remove bone, put on greased tin, stuff, place rashers on top and cook for thirty minutes. Stuff tomatoes. Wash up. Set table. Put serving dishes in to heat. Cream the potatoes. Add eggs. Look at fish. Sieve sauce, put to heat gently. Prepare garnish. Take out fish and keep hot. Take out tomatoes and tidy up. Serve up. Wash up. The instructions for an invisible life serving others. And it did sum up her life. A public display of serving others with no hint of her own self in the picture, because she was tireless in her efforts to attend to her husband's needs and her children's needs.

'You do your best,' she'd say, 'but you get no thanks.'

There was a cooking competition and she won first prize. I remember helping her bring pots and pans and cutlery into the schoolhouse where the competition was held on the day of the finals. I was six years old and stood among the frocked haunches of other women squeezing me out of sight as they leaned in for the judge's decisions, and I desperately wished for my mother to win. And she did. And my pride in her was beyond control that she could beat all those other enormous perfumed ladies. I remember seeing her smile and holding the prize, a little silver cup. And I held a photograph of that too, as I foraged under the stairs.

I found a letter from the President of Ireland, Paddy Hillery, sympathising with her on the death of her brother Oliver, and a letter from the head gardener at Áras an Uachtaráin. And with them, another photograph of Oliver and her, arm in arm outside the front door of his house, and the entire list of mourners at his funeral. That museum of her unconscious mind held me transfixed.

Sometimes as a child, I used to go upstairs and cry alone

in the bathroom while I was looking in the mirror. Don't ask me why. I was drawn to mirrors. I spent hours in front of every mirror in the house. And there were a lot of them. On the dressing table of every bedroom and inside the doors of every wardrobe. And I was never caught. I was far too careful because adults didn't approve of children looking in mirrors for too long. They said if you looked long enough in the mirror you might see the devil. Although the one I was terrified of was Dracula. I always feared that he might suddenly stare out at me with his fangs and lips of blood and point at me and say, 'It's time for your check-up.'

It was at the mirror that I first began talking to myself. I'd chastise myself as if I was the schoolteacher and the fellow in the mirror was someone else. Mother would hear me and call me down.

'What were you doing in my room?' she would ask, and I would make something up, because lies come fast to the unconscious mind.

'I was looking for matches,' I might say, since the fire might need to be lit and there was usually a box of matches sitting on the shelf between the statue of the Virgin Mary and the nightlight that she lit when she was going to bed.

The wonderful thing about life now is that there is no shame at all in being paralysed by narcissism. Teenagers on the streets are constantly looking sideways as they walk, admiring their own faces in the passing shop windows. But I suppose they're only doing in public what I did in secret

143

before the mirror. And I love the way they look out at me sometimes with gleeful faces from their Facebook pages. They smile as if nothing in the world was bothering them. As if they were not terrified of ever being alone, or not desiring madly to be held.

In my mother's day, young people looked into cameras with a similar exuberance. At least that's how she looks in old photographs from Cork. But maybe she too mooched about the rooms of her new home in Cavan after she was married and looked in the same mirrors and talked quietly to herself about how her new married life was getting along. At least all the mirrors were still intact, when I was examining the place like a forensic detective after she died. At one point I looked intently into the long oblong mirror in the bathroom just over the wash-hand basin, and I could still see the remnant of the child I once was staring back at me.

144   I still stare at mirrors. In the washrooms of five-star hotels or on the corridors of leisure centres or just in the gleaming glass of shop windows where I do what teenagers do.

I remember taking my mother to the Brandon Hotel in Tralee for a holiday just after my father's death. She was reluctant, and still heavy with grief when we set out from Cavan, but as we moved down through the lush woodlands of Offaly and Limerick, the white hawthorn and the flag irises cheered her up and by the time we got through Adare with its thatched cottages and arrived in Kerry, it was me who was falling into depression and she who was growing more delighted.

And I was the one absorbed by my own image in the lift mirror after we had checked in. She just kept her eye on the lift door, like a child waiting for it to open and release her onto the corridor of the third floor where we had been assigned our bedrooms.

Even in old age, she still had an insatiable desire to connect with other people, as if she had no inner self. As if no conscious part of her mind was watching. She lived completely in the acting out of her engagement with the world, like those cheerful little girls on Facebook. The next person to turn up at her door was always a more exciting prospect than sitting with her own anxieties – which is why it was all so devastating for her in the end. And why the silent doorbell and the phone that never rang broke her heart in old age, and why, when depression came, it came with a vengeance. At ninety, no one called. And she grew bitter. And she never shared with me the regrets that afflicted her in that uneasy solitude.

AS I HEADED up the stairs of her house on Farnham Road, I was still looking for her, still wanting her presence to rise from some accidental artefact. My destination was the upstairs bedroom. So on I went, slowly, treading the dull brown carpet on the stairs, stained from various accidents over the years. I passed the icon of the Virgin Mary at the turn in the stairs. An icon which I had bought at a stall outside Christ Church Cathedral when Brother Roger of Taizé was in Dublin in 1983, and which, whenever I looked at it, made me sad.

I had driven a bus full of young people from troubled backgrounds in Fermanagh to see the holy monk and, at one stage, he passed close to us as we stood in the porch with hundreds of others. The frail white-haired man was being escorted out of the cathedral after he had delivered his sermon. Someone in the crowd said we were from Northern Ireland and he came over and hugged all the young people individually and each one cried, and then he looked at me, standing at a remove, and he said, 'You are a priest.' I didn't know if he was asking me a question or declaring some truth, and I'm not quite sure what I said in reply but I too was embraced and I too cried.

Less than a year later, I had left the ministry but I didn't have the heart to throw out the icon, so I gave it to my mother and it hung on the wall in Cavan between downstairs and the upstairs landing, and often in the years after I had abandoned the priesthood, when I was visiting her and might have occasion to go to the toilet, I would see it on the wall and be caught by a sudden sense of remorse.

The bed in the dining room had been a temporary solution and had only been in operation for two years. It was a public place where the nurses and the care workers came and went during her last years in the house. But upstairs was different. It was private. I opened her bedroom door and was immediately held by her presence more powerfully than in any other room. This was the room where my father had slept with her. Where I was conceived. Where he grew old, lying on the bed, listening to BBC Radio 4 and gazing out at the evening sun, and saying to me that heaven might be a state of bliss, a nowhere land where everything beautiful we had in this world might be experienced again, and even then more intensely.

Upstairs is where she dreamed, the room where she made love and then grew old. And it is the room where I was born. I felt shame as I poked about in the drawers and rummaged in her wardrobe and stood staring at her bed and dressing table and all the idle brushes and combs and silver mirrors. She spent over twenty years in that room with her husband. And for thirty more years, she slept in the same bed alone as a widow.

In my childhood, mother wore frocks and dresses and light-blue mohair cardigans around her shoulders, and strings of pearls down along her bodice. I remember her wearing dainty hats with feathers sticking up, and black patent shoes. And I'll never forget the night I saw her in a black strapless evening gown swishing in circles at the mirror, in anticipation of a night's dancing and drinking and the whizz of posh gossip.

I remember going to a film in the Magnet Cinema in Cavan when I was very young and seeing a slim woman on the screen, in a long raincoat belted at the waist and a scarf hiding her hair; she was standing in a doorway in some black-and-white thriller. In the next scene, the door opened and she went inside and took off the wet coat and the scarf and

148

a strange man with a moustache threw a cardigan around her shoulders and she sat down and leaned her elbow on a dining table, and I trembled with astonishment. I thought it was her. I thought it was Mammy. My own film star mammy in one of her perfect frocks. And I knew where frocks came from because I remember going regularly to a dressmaker's house on Church Street with her. We would go upstairs to the fitting room. The dressmaker, Miss Brady, was old by then, and had been making and altering clothes for Mother since Mother was a child. There too, with just the three of us in the room, I can recall sitting on the floor watching her swish around at the mirror, so lovely to behold.

Those were the days when I was enraptured by her joy and her capabilities, and I loved every moment in her company.

Every Sunday of my childhood, my mother boiled a chicken in the same manner as her mother had taught her. 149 If there was anything that signalled to me my mother's love and affection, it was the taste of chicken soup.

I was six when she learned to drive my father's Austin A40 and I remember sitting in the passenger seat after school one particular Friday afternoon when she took me with her to do the weekly messages. Firstly she collected the groceries in town as usual, calling to Baxter's chemist, Foster's newsagent and providers on Main Street, where the men behind the counter like Mr Dolan had brown overcoats and could wrap twine round brown paper parcels of cold meat or loaves of bread and then snap the twine apart with a flick of their fingers. She went to the butcher, a huge, tall man with enormous hands, who stood behind his chopping block of bone and flesh and who said the same thing every week.

'Is this the youngest one, Nellie?' And I would bow my head and stare at the sawdust on the floor as they discussed whom I looked like.

Then we drove seven winding miles out the narrow roads to the creamery in Ballyhaise where boys in white coats and little white hats filled one can with cream and another one with buttermilk, and she walked across the road to the Agricultural College to buy eggs and fresh vegetables from the farm shop. Finally on our way back, she turned in the gates of Reilly's farm near Crossdoney and drove up a long avenue of beech trees into a broad, grey concrete yard. The yard was as busy as an industrial zone with trailers of animal feed coming and going, and huge cages of chickens and half a dozen helpers in wellingtons and blue overalls, and gated pens of chickens in every corner and a long, grey galvanised shed with enormous sliding doors at the far end.

'That's where the chickens are,' Mother said, although there were chickens everywhere. 'It's where they hang the dead ones,' she explained.

I was getting a bit uneasy so I just flicked through the

Beano while Mother watched Mr Reilly, a lanky old man with white hair, stride across the yard towards the car.

'Nellie Finlay,' he said, 'it's great to see you. That's a cold day.'

'How is Helen?' my mother enquired.

'She's home,' he said. 'Why don't you go inside and say hello?'

I guessed Helen must be his wife and she may have been in hospital.

'I don't want to be disturbing her. She has her hands full with the baby.'

'Yerra go on,' he said, almost shouting with joy. 'She'd love to see you.'

And so Mother decided to go in and have a cup of tea. But she wasn't sure what to do with me for the moment.

'The little man can help me find a chicken,' Mr Reilly suggested.

A cigarette hung from the side of his mouth. He wore braces over a blue shirt and black trousers stuffed into hob-nailed boots.

'Go in and have tea, I'm telling you,' he repeated, 'and leave the little man to me. I'll show him the chickens.'

'But I can see the chickens from here,' I said, still in the car and thinking that it would be better to stay with the *Beano* than go traipsing into unknown territories with the lanky, chain-smoking Mr Reilly.

'She'll be only delighted to see Nellie Finlay. Go in, will

151

you, for God's sake.' It felt like she was being asked to go and have tea on the moon. Although Mr Reilly seemed very determined that she'd go inside. He always called my mother Nellie Finlay. It was her name before she married and I guessed they'd known each other since they were young.

Then he turned to me and said, 'Now, young lad, do you want to see the chickens?'

I could see hundreds of chickens, many of whom had surrounded the grey Austin A40 as if they too might have an interest in the *Beano*.

'Has your wife had a baby?' I asked, with childlike intuition.

He doubled over with laughter. Then he stopped suddenly, and was very still and eyeballed me through the window.

'Wife's long dead,' he whispered, with an expressionless face. 'The light of heaven to her.'

He opened the door of the car as if to force me out.

'Helen is my daughter. And, yes, she's just had a baby. Now, come on.'

He turned on his heel and I followed as he led me towards the shed where he hefted the sliding door open and we walked into a vast darkness full of dead things, hung from hooks on endless lines. They were naked and wrinkled like an old man's neck, hanging upside down by strings tied to their yellow claws, their heads bloated from the blood that had drained downwards from their bodies. I speculated on the manner of their execution as I followed Mr Reilly's jaunty step down one aisle and up another between the endless rows; a thousand dead birds on either side, but I was too afraid to speak.

'What would you like?' he asked.

'A boiling fowl,' I said.

'A boiler,' he said.

'She wants a nice young boiling fowl,' I repeated, just as my mother would say it.

'She does indeed,' he said. 'The young birds are tender. Isn't that the truth?'

'Aye, that's the truth,' I said, affecting a rustic disposition that seemed appropriate.

And off he went down another aisle humming 'Love Me Tender', with a cleaving knife swinging from his left hand.

And then he spotted one.

'Here she is,' he said. And he lifted a little pullet off its hook, his knife in one hand and the bird swinging in the other as he went to a table back near the door where with one chop he took the head off and swept it into a steel bin.

'Will she take the gizzard?' he wondered.

'Oh, aye,' I said, 'for the soup.'

'For the soup exactly,' he repeated, because he was only humouring me with questions. 'Sure you can't make soup without the gizzard. And the neck?' he wondered. 'Does she want the neck?'

153

'Aye, she does,' I said. 'The neck and the gizzard please.'

These things he put aside when he was cleaning the bird; slicing and pulling and flinging the slops into the bin. He chopped the legs off with another single stroke of the cleaver and approached me with the claws.

'D'ye want these?' he asked, as he pulled a tendon that made the little claws open and close. I took them from him and pressed them into my coat pocket and I couldn't wait to be back in the car with Mother so that I could show them to her.

When she died, her clothes were a consolation. I touched them, held them, hugged them, and inhaled from them the remnant of the feminine beauty that had once seduced my father. I sat on her bed, and looked out the window for ages. Then I opened a drawer in her dressing table and was overwhelmed by a sense of intense intimacy. The puff of air still carried something from long ago. It was like a sudden memory and the image of a satin purse flashed through my mind and immediately I went rummaging for it in every drawer in the room.

In photos she is always slim; a young woman bursting out of her skin with excitement. I loved all her clothes. Her red coats, her flower-patterned frocks belted tight at the waist and her cute skullcaps with white feathers. She smiled with outrageous confidence at every camera. As an old woman, she had worn conservative suits in more restrained colours, and understated, low-heeled footwear. Almost everything was still in the room, folded neatly, tucked into drawers or hanging on clothes hangers. But it was her purse I wanted. And I rummaged through the wardrobes with a desperate longing to find it again – vivid and fresh and soft. A black satin purse with a black bow at the top and two golden clasps that clipped it shut.

I remember the night she went out in the black dress with no straps. The dress that spread out at the hem and was trimmed with purple velvet ribbons, and she held this purse and clasped it shut and, as she turned around to say goodnight, I knew she was happy, the tiny black feathery cap on her head, her eyes dramatically dark and lined with black pencil. I had seen her draw the lines with the delicacy of a painter. I had leaned over her shoulder and stared into the mirror as the pencil slid across her eyelid. She kissed me goodnight and I tasted her lipstick. I was only six. And then, over fifty years later, in the bottom of a wardrobe, up from under the layers of old coats and high-heeled shoes and feather pillows it came, the little purse, soft as a sleeping thrush, back to my fingertips and I felt shameful touching it and my face reddened with a delicious pleasure.

I always dreamed that my mother's dressmaker would make me something to wear too. She seemed to bring such gladness into my mother's heart with her scissors and her pins and her needle and thread. But the tailor I was sent to for Communion or Confirmation suits was a mournful old man with a bald head. When I was heading for the seminary to study for the priesthood, he made me a soutane, a long black frock that buttoned at the front from chin to toe. It felt like being fitted for a shroud. The letter from the seminary said that an umbrella and a hat were also essential requirements. I stood in the tailor's shop among the dummies and the long rolls of black wool on the counter as the tailor knelt between my legs and pinned stripes of white paper to the inside of my trouser leg, and underneath my arms. His spectacles were balanced on the edge of his nose and he was holding a bunch of pins between his lips.

'You don't look very happy,' he muttered.

I wasn't. But I thought it might have cheered my mother up to see me dressed in a long black cassock. And eventually it did.

When I was ordained a priest ten years later, Mother came with me to the parish, and she was over the moon about having a son in the clergy. They might as well have ordained the two of us. She was actually better at the job than I was. When I worked as a parish curate in Fermanagh, she came to visit every weekend, and answered any ring at the front door as if she was running the show, and her clothes sense was certain and confident. She was in her late sixties by then. A hand-knitted green cardigan with Celtic patterns and a navy brown tweed skirt. Gold on her wrists and around her neck and her earlobes adorned with pearls, her thin feminine frame, the lightness of her feet and her gracious smile surprising whatever poor soul stood in the porch, in a scarf and overcoat, clasping five pounds, and a mass card for the priest to sign.

One Sunday morning, a young man in extreme depression came to the door at nine o'clock. We sat in the front room for an hour as I listened to his woes and Mother swept the hall outside. He lay limp in an armchair, sharing his anxieties, and he was almost catatonic from the power of melancholy. I needed to go and celebrate Sunday mass, so I told him to stay where he was until I got back. The truth is that even as a priest I was more confused than he was about the meaning of life, so I was going to be of no help to him at all apart from referring him to some professional counsellor. In the kitchen, I spoke to my mother.

'Make him some tea, but don't go near him and I'll try to find someone who can help later in the morning.'

When I returned she was sitting with him, in full flight about how much mothers worry about their children. In fairness, he was smiling and I marvelled at her capacity as a therapist. Though she was sitting on the opposite armchair, she was, in a sense, holding him, deeply and intimately. I might as well have been watching a therapist from uptown New York. And she was wearing that elegant green cardigan, the same cardigan that dangled from a hanger in her wardrobe with everything else after she died.

Perhaps I needed someone who didn't know her to come and clean up all that mess in her house; to take the clothes to a charity shop and throw everything else in a skip and then the job would be done. But I couldn't hear of it. She was a month dead, but this museum of her unconscious mind, this catalogue of her desires, disappointments and secrets, constituted a fabric of broken energy that entangled me and that I carried with me through life, and I alone could disentangle myself and dismantle her web. After all, she was my mother. I looked again at the combs on the dressing table. There were strands of grey hair in the teeth. I took up a silver brush and kissed the back of it. It was getting dark outside, but I didn't want to leave.

I remember going to see her on Christmas morning in 2011. I passed through the nursing home, smiling at the staff. The corridors were warm and cosy, although outside there was snow on the ground and ice-blue skies over the canal. My mother, and her elderly companions, were wheeled into the day room with great fuss and fanfare.

Bald heads dappled in the winter sunlight turned to examine me. Withered eyes squinted at the Christmas tree and the colourful lights and the presents that the staff distributed. Later when a musician arrived, everyone danced, even my mother, who was in a wheelchair. Though she didn't really know what day it was. She clutched the handbag in which she kept everything that mattered: her photographs, her rings, her chequebook and other remnants of the past. Times when her husband was young and they danced on New Year's Eve at the golf club. Times when her

158

children were small and she baked Christmas cakes, and puddings, and arranged precious baubles on the Christmas tree to amaze them. She was wearing a scarf that we had brought her that morning as a gift, though she paid it little attention. She just closed her eyes and opened her eyes. And breathed in and out. That was about it. Her companions were looking great. Nurses had helped to powder noses, and apply lipstick and make-up, and there was a tint of colour and a lively shape in everyone's hair, thanks to Majella the hairdresser who had called in a few days earlier. Then came the Christmas dinner and all the good china and the paper hats and my mother looked bewildered as she stared at the Christmas pudding and the pot of coffee.

'Oh, look,' she said, 'isn't that a beautiful teapot.'

When she went to Irish Countrywomen's Association meetings on winter nights I used to walk with her into town. There she joined other housewives with permed hair behind a closed door and drank tea from an exquisite china teapot on the second floor of Tower Hamlet, a creaking, eighteenth-century building in the middle of town, while I played on the stairs and buried myself in the ladies' overcoats that hung on the wall hooks.

While we were out, my father would get a notion to reposition the furniture or rearrange the paintings on the walls. But she never quite understood what he was doing because he always made a mess of it. There was a lack of refinement in him which disabled any intelligent engagement with the sensate world, and that appalled her. He was a talking man, a wordy man. Her own arrangement of furniture was unconscious and always artistic. Even with her eyes closed, she could make things lovely, whether it was a tray of meringues in the oven or the arrangement of flowers in a vase. There was a natural aesthetic at play when she gathered little ornaments and objects around her. Her emotions were never verbalised. Her story was never told. But the interior of her house held it all. The museum of useless stuff she left in her wake was as eloquent as a novel.

As I looked into the back bedroom, the final room I examined, I felt exhausted. And for no particular reason, I lay down on the bed, allowing myself to be swallowed up in waking dreams for half an hour, intending then to rise and leave and drive home. But sleep overtook me like a tide, and I drifted into that unconscious state which was the only place where I could still speak with her.

At first, I dreamed about Brahma, the Hindu god who creates everything that exists from sound, each universe from the vibration of his breath. He simply breathes out. And breathes in. And then closes his eyes. And falls asleep. And then he wakes up. And opens his eyes. And breathes out again. And then he breathes in. And he closes his eyes. And thus the universe pulses for eternity. And that was my mother's rhythm too, before she died. Every few minutes, she woke up and opened her eyes. Then she closed her eyes. And fell asleep again. And then she woke again. I think it was the house that made me dream like that. It too had a pulse. It had lungs, and I could feel it breathing all around me. I was conscious of the fact that sixty years earlier I had been born in that same room, in that same little house of my mother's broken dreams.

So there I was on Farnham Road in Cavan, dreaming of everything mad, from Hindu gods and thrushes to Russian snow and the Queen of England. All night, I talked with her in dreams as soft as a bog that enfolds itself around the ashes of old fires, and the hearthstones of ancient houses, and the butter that was churned a thousand years ago and the wizened leather faces of the dead. And I slept until dawn when I heard the birds again in the attic and under the eaves of the house.

THE MORNING AFTER I shared my curry with the cat, the wind was gusting and the ground was dry. I stood at the gable of my studio listening to my five stones; they were smooth and round and as big as ostrich eggs and sat one on top of the other on the step of the studio. I believe that if I make offerings to my own demons regularly, I can keep them under control. Anger, rage, jealousy and all the other disturbing emotions a human being experiences between one sup of tea and the next can be personified, and assigned a particular corner of the garden, and kept at bay with generous offerings of breadcrumbs, bowls of water, jelly beans or wild flowers. My therapist thought I was nuts, but what can you say to the unbelieving? When you respect your darkest energy, like anger, and when you are mindful of it, and when you hold and embrace it, then you're less likely to be possessed by it unconsciously. That's what I believe. So the stones became a kind of shrine to my demons. I would leave peanuts beside them, which the birds enjoyed through the winter, and sometimes I even imagined that the wind faintly whistling through the stones was the sound of those demons in pain and I felt pity for them.

A few days after I threw the stone at the magpie and hit the postman, he came again, this time to the studio, and caught me reverently placing a jelly baby sweet on top of the stones.

'What's all this about?' the postman wondered.

'I like to feed the birds,' I said, not wanting to share with him the real intent of my ritual in case he'd be frightened away and I'd never get any more letters.

'Didn't know they liked sweets,' he said suspiciously.

'Oh, yes,' I assured him, 'some of them are mad for the jelly babies.'

But these rituals, like everything else in the ornate world of Buddhist practice, were, as far as I was concerned, merely a method of becoming more conscious of the disturbing emotions that drew me into depression. By doing this yoga of conscious activity, I tried to protect myself from ever becoming completely possessed by them.

Not that the person who gave me the stones shared any of these fanciful notions. She just presented them for my birthday a month after my mother died because she found them on the beach and thought them to be pretty and eloquent and I was delighted with her generous gift. That was back in August 2012. They were oval and they held fossils on their surface, and they could be arranged in stacks. The smaller stones sat on top of the larger ones and they made two small monuments. But to assemble them outside the door of my new studio like a shrine was my own idea.

I used to sit by the fire and stare at them through the window, and I remember one day in September falling asleep so that when my beloved arrived, she laughed.

'Well, just look at the old man dozing by the fire,' she said.

I said, 'I'm lucky to have a fire, considering the price of coal and the carbon tax, and the number of windmills all around me now, whose owners are granted enormous sums of taxpayers' money just to lodge those monstrous cement creatures on what used to be the bare and beautiful slopes of lovely Leitrim.'

'There he goes again,' she said, 'the old man is growing bitter.'

I confided in her how I was hoping to hear the wind

whistle through the stones. She said she didn't think that the wind would make any noise. I said it did at the gable wall. 'But those stones are too small,' she said, 'to deflect the wind in a manner that might create music.'

I said, 'A boiling kettle makes music too.'

To which she said, 'OK, I get the message. I'll make some tea.' And she turned to go back into the house.

'I'll follow you in a few moments,' I said, but I didn't. I forgot. Or perhaps I fell asleep again.

It was like that during the autumn. We lived placidly in the hills. I mourned quietly in my newly built room at the back of the house, looking out over Lough Allen. Across the wide water I could see Sliabh an Iarainn and the mountains of west Cavan, the lakes and small fields, and the forests and bogs.

L IKE MANY OTHER artists, I arrived in Leitrim in the 1980s, not just because of a black economy and cheap housing, but because we were all seeking some spiritual holy ground. Germans came. Painters. Writers. Sculptors. They bought up little cottages very cheaply. Many were refugees from broken homes, dysfunctional families or unresolved relationships; like one-winged birds seeking shelter in a ditch.

I settled on the Leitrim–Roscommon border after years

of wandering around west Donegal, south Fermanagh and east Galway, renting bungalows or chalets in remote corners of the countryside.

I once passed a winter on a wild headland near Annagry in Donegal, just to watch the ocean beat off the rocks in the moonlight. To listen in the morning to the waves of the sea break on the beach at Carrickfinn.

And there were hills around Lough Allen where I once walked a dog; hills as barren as the moon. The road curling up into the high ground beyond the village, where the wind screeched through empty mineshafts and over bare slag heaps; mounds of rock and shale and shifted earth, a graveyard of dead diggers and mining machinery. Bleak highways cut into the mountain, to make a path for wind turbines that arrived with the new century on lorries as big as any Yankee convoy in Kabul.

The first time I heard the sound of a curlew, I thought it so forlorn that it sucked all my neurosis out, and left me as clean as an empty bowl. Wilderness, I believed, was the mother of all poetry.

There was a nineteenth-century notion that if you got away to the wilds, you could find your wildness. If you got to a space with no fences, then your mind would be without boundaries. Romantic poets could let loose their creativity, if they but owned a little cottage in a bee-loud glade or went fishing at midnight in a boat on Lough Erne, seeking pike by the light of a moon. In England,

Wordsworth wallowed in a rustic romance of daffodils, pretty girls sweating in the fields, and brooding mountains. But it was Yeats who forged the template for Romantic Ireland, in misty bogs where ancient heroes wandered and the wind whistled through stones where fairies sang. And we know where all that led; Europeans in dungarees with albums by Clannad and dilated eyeballs, trying to lure the Shee off Bohey Mountain with tin whistles.

I found it possible to be human in rural Ireland, far away from the suburban lawns of Farnham Road. I had fled from a middle-class childhood, a world of manners and decorum, and found a kind of serenity in the wilderness of boggy mountain, lake and river. This is where I could brood in solitude and safety, lick my wounds and absorb the healing energy of the earth and sky.

Living on the side of a mountain seemed like a healthier option for the spirit, when compared to what cities offered. I got a wide view up in the mountains. I got close to the stars at night. I got close to goats in the daylight. I lived in the wind and was wrapped in leaves. There was something ancient about the routine of daily life in the country. People sat in the kitchen listening to the clock. They could hear footsteps on the laneway when someone was half a mile away. They could tell the emotions of animals. They told stories and gossiped about things that happened a hundred years ago. It all implied that no mountain was as wonderful as their mountain. No place was as special as their place.

They knew what was going to happen next, though usually nothing happened.

And, of course, they were never alone. They sat deeply in the world. They walked deeply on the surface of Mother Earth. When they uttered the names of townlands, it was as if they were invoking some real presence: Gubaveeny, Éadan Mór or Coratavvy.

If the doctor asked an old man in the waiting room for his name, he might say, 'Jack So-and-so from Altacorran [or wherever]' because to speak his surname in isolation was not quite adequate a description. Only when a person was placed within the matrix of all the love and sorrow of his people – their deaths and poverty and heroic deeds that a single townland name could conjure up – was he properly defined as human.

In dancehalls sometimes in those old days, a girl might ask a boy where he was from and he would utter his townland name and she would look through him as if she were seeing all the strings that held him to his people and made him the 'Who' that she wanted to hold.

That September, when I walked up the hilly road along the wild ravines of Arigna and across the shoulders of the mountain, I could hear a sound deep in the rocks, like clear bells, and more real than my own voice. I could hear a kind of music vibrating in the trees, the wind playing sonatas in the forestry, mimicking the sound of a Japanese flute. And when my mother had been buried on a small hill in

Cavan, I returned to Arigna and spent weeks walking the hills and sitting in my studio nursing grief and listening to the stones singing in the wind. I lit the fire. I stared out at the lake. I began reading Chinese poetry and hoped that autumn would be a time of recovery from the grief and emptiness I felt since her death.

After lunch each day, I would say to my beloved in the kitchen that I was going to work. I would leave the house, go to the end of the yard and enter my room, where I would stretch out on an armchair and doze.

Like the Chinese poet Po Chu-I, who lived over a thousand years ago, I abandoned myself to dreams for some of the afternoon and then drank bowls of tea and, just like him, I took heed of the lengthening shadows of evening. I could almost hear him whispering to me.

'Winter is coming. Winter is coming. Joyful people regret the fleeting years, and sad people must endure the slow hours, but only those without joy or sorrow can accept what life brings. Winter is coming.'

IN THE DAYS after I had thrown the stone at the postman I began to realise that I'm one of those men who doesn't improve on their own. I get locked into solitude in a lazy sort of way. Like the way a moth circles a flame. Maybe it's the sterility of the male psyche, or the lack of a womb, that gives us the propensity to sit idle for hours, barely conscious of the fact that we are alive and yet transfixed by the certainty of being extinguished in death. Over the years, men have conjured up an endless number of metaphysical concepts that ease the pain of this existential anxiety, from God and Buddha to a wide variety of New-Age substitutes. Men, as someone once said, have all the answers but very few of the questions.

On Midsummer's Eve, the mountains in the west of Ireland hum with the sounds of the New Age; the pulse and beat of drums, and the cry of shamans connecting with their animal souls, and a wide variety of alternative political and social activists seeking converts on the streets of various arts festivals. Catholicism may have crumbled, but the fervour of men who passionately believe in odd forms of metaphysical truth still continues. Just leave a man alone for long enough west of the Shannon river and he will discover the meaning of life. And then he'll try to convince everyone else that he is the one with the right answer.

But it was conventional religion that was my weakness. I grew up in the house of Catholic iconography and I could never quite let go of it. And even now I remain religious. I can't let go of the sense that my Self belongs in the deep otherness of an infinite cosmos. I can't let go of the consolation that fading into the universe at death might be natural and that death may hold the greatest possibility of all. And what draws me into that? I don't know. Maybe it's a man thing. Or maybe it's a fear-of-death thing. Or maybe it's just the utter poetry of it.

But when the beloved was in Poland, I had no one to discuss all this with except the cat. Day by day, I nurtured the same fanciful ideas and exotic notions regarding the various reincarnations of myself and my little pussy. From one lifetime to the next she may have been sticking to me just to help me towards the enlightenment she already enjoyed. She may have been incarnating as a cat just to allow me find in myself compassion for cats. After all, she was calmer than me. And I became even more convinced than ever that she may have been an abbess long ago when I was just a humble monk, and when we were both drenched to the bone on Skellig Michael or some other remote refuge, hunting together for fish and enlightenment.

The pattern continued every day. Some mornings I would go with the flow and lie in bed. The next morning I would get up and go walking in the hills like a wise man or a fool, and I would return after perhaps two hours and light a candle and sit in single-pointed concentration in my studio.

And I assured myself that to be enlightened was to go with every flow. So when I wanted to eat buns or cheese sandwiches or drink espresso I went to the kitchen and filled my belly, pleasuring myself in the security that I was not pleasuring myself at all. I ate chocolate at the television at night, assuring myself that I was not attached to it. The chocolate was of no significance to me; in fact it would have been unenlightened to resist it. I suppose once you establish that you're in tune with the Lord of the entire universe, there is no end to the possibilities of self-delusion.

And I'll never be able to resist candles – lighting them, gazing at them – sitting there thinking that I am loved by a mother who is hidden behind the veil of the natural world. Other men get up to all sorts of strange things while they are alone. They watch porn or sports channels or find women to whom they can tell lies in the hope of sexual gratification. They probably have far more fun than I do. But at least I had the freedom to do as I pleased, even if I only wanted to sit still and watch the tiny flickering flame.

All that would change when she returned. She would say, 'Come home to reality, my love. Awaken to this present moment. It is our time. Soon it will be summer and the grass will need to be cut, my love. The smell of mown lawns will envelop us.'

She would gaze at me again, like the sun shining, and I would smile. I dreamed one night of a couple of otters lying on the surface of a river, holding each other's hands as they slept in case they might slip apart and lose each other in the current. It was a dream that consoled me and made me feel I was not a stranger walking on the earth.

But while she was away, the pond had filled with frogspawn. The hares had begun wandering the fields like they owned the world. The badgers were down in the warrens near the quarry, minding their newly born babies. The magpies were watching for movements in the house in the hope that I might soon throw out some organic material. The crows were getting ready to build.

Each morning, the sun rose a little earlier over Leitrim, over the houses in Drumshanbo, and the new apartments in Carrick-on-Shannon, and the cottages around Manorhamilton where the artists slept, and the polythene benders and tents in the ditches where the New-Age hippies sheltered while they tried to retrieve their souls and find pathways in the undergrowth to some lost paradise. And the sun cast its morning light indifferently on the living and the dead. On the commuters heading to work in factories and hardware stores and the county council offices, and across the graves of musicians and poets and teenagers killed on the roads or in fatal accidents around the farm or on building sites in London. The sun cast its light on John McGahern's grave, and on the grave of a bishop who once ordered a local library to remove all McGahern's books from the shelves, and all the other sleeping dead in graveyards of every parish and village in this quiet county.

Sixty years ago, when I had just been born, Leitrim was a land of poor soil where the crack of a spade on stony ground could be heard through the still air from distant fields. But now it had been reinvented by a new generation – sculptors and painters and ceramic artists and film-makers and wood carvers and actors and even old IRA veterans who had built new lives with cross-border grants and retired guards and hippies from London and playwrights and old farmers whose sons were gay and lived in Brooklyn. The power of the clergy had greatly diminished, though there were still a few priests who would rise early in the morning and sleep in the afternoons, and other priests who didn't get out of bed until noon, and ex-priests who couldn't sleep at all.

Everything changes. Nothing is permanent. So for the time being, there are fewer priests in Leitrim but more lesbians, fewer bank managers but more musicians. But who can tell what lies in the future?

As I looked out from my hilltop cottage in the hills above Lough Allen, overlooking the mountains that stretch from the peaks of Cuilce to the slopes of Sliabh an Iarainn near Drumshanbo, I could assure myself that, for this time being, Leitrim was undoubtedly an auspicious place to live.

I T WAS NINE o'clock on a Monday morning when he phoned me, the beginning of my third week alone. The rain was beating the roof and the windows on the west side of the cottage. I went to the kitchen and settled a few scoops of coffee in a small espresso pot and placed it on a hot ring. I even resisted putting a bowl of porridge flakes in the microwave now that I was on the verge of becoming an enlightened Buddha, given that Buddhas don't need porridge, as far as I know. I turned on the radio and then turned it off. I drank the coffee and went outside for a brief investigation of the compound. The trees were bending in the westerly wind but none had fallen. Lough Allen was all tossed up by the storm and the white waves dotted the length of it, and some of the islands seemed to have shrunk in size, as the flood levels in the lake rose higher. A guttering had collapsed on one side of the cottage, and the water tank was overflowing and creating a pool of water beyond the east gable. I came back inside and saw for the first time a stain on the ceiling of the kitchen where water must have come in under the tiles and saturated the insulation in the attic. This didn't alarm me because I knew we had a loose tile on that side. But then I saw another larger and darker brown stain on the ceiling around where the chimney takes the smoke and heat from the range up through the roof. And then I saw a stain on the wall, down along the chimney breast. In panic, I went into the next room and there too I noticed brown stains seeping through the white paint of the ceiling. I went to the sun room, where the ceiling was sagging like a hammock in the centre.

This is not good, I thought.

And then the phone rang. I didn't recognise the number and at first I didn't recognise the voice.

'Is that yourself?' he asked.

'Who else would it be?' I said.

He laughed.

'It's me,' he said.

'Good,' I replied. 'I thought it was you.'

'So how are you?'

'I'm fine. But who are you?'

'This is Enda,' he said.

'Right.'

'Enda Maguire.'

'Ohhhhhh, Enda Maguire. Well, how are you? We studied in Maynooth. Yes, I remember you. Did you ever get ordained afterwards?'

'I didn't. I got married.'

'Good,' I said. 'Much better.'

'I'm ringing about Tom Lunny.'

Tom Lunny was a parish priest in Laois when we were students in Maynooth and he was our hero. He loved theatre, T.S. Eliot and Verdi operas. He was a liberal, but also irrational and socially dysfunctional. For example, he couldn't stand nuns and sometimes insulted them at mass by refusing to allow them to give out Communion. On one occasion when an overenthusiastic young woman in a veil walked over to him at the sign of peace with her arms outstretched, he whispered, 'Feic off, Noddy,' and then for no apparent reason he turned his back against her gesture of compassion.

'A liberal indeed, but not a man to be sentimental about women,' I suggested.

'No, indeed,' Enda said down the telephone.

'I remember he once described charismatic prayer meetings as a rash on the mystical body of Christ.'

'He's dead,' Enda said.

'Right,' I answered. 'I suppose we all die sometimes. Buddhists say it's in our nature to die. Should be good for us.'

'The funeral is tomorrow.'

'It's for the best,' I said. 'No point in leaving him above ground going stale. He'll want his body for the resurrection.'

'For fuck's sake,' Enda said, 'you're being a prick.'

'Sorry,' I said, 'sometimes I don't realise how cynical the past thirty years of clerical scandals has left me. I think there's a scar on my psyche.'

'I was just wondering,' he said, 'would you be going to the funeral? Seeing as how he was such a support to you and me when we were students.'

'You must be joking,' I said.

Tom Lunny's head was shaved like an American marine and he had a deep voice, though he was never without his packet of Marlboro which he enjoyed with leisurely gestures, exhaling jets of blue smoke between his sentences. His shaved neck was beetroot red, and he had big ears that stuck out – perpendicular – to the sides of his head, and eyebrows as bushy as small mice. His lower lip was thick and purple, and he could hold the filter of the cigarette between his teeth with an uneasy sensuality. Everything about him was a contradiction; he was like a cross between a farmer from Limerick and Ernest Hemingway. He was ten years our senior but he'd often come to the seminary and we'd go out drinking, to shaded corners of the Roost on Main Street or sometimes to bars around Grafton Street in Dublin where we laughed together and talked about some theatre show we had just seen at the Focus, or liberation theology and the possibilities of love in the barrios of South America. He impressed us because though he was older, he seemed very modern and confident. He was a philosopher. A man so disinclined to partake in ritual that you'd wonder how he sustained himself as a parish priest in Ireland for all those years.

Sometimes he'd agree to stay over in the seminary, and we'd end up in a room in Dunboyne House where he lodged himself, drinking whiskey. And when the bottle was finished and we were preparing the mugs of instant coffee, he'd suddenly declare that he had to go.

'Well, fuck me, boys, I just realised I have a funeral at ten in the morning,' he'd say, and he'd get into his car, at maybe 3 a.m., and head out the gates and off down the country towards his parish at the far end of Laois.

But he wasn't unusual. The Church in the 1970s was a divided city. Some clerics slept with women. Some clerics had gay relationships. Women slipped in and out of the parochial houses by night. Old conservative bishops patrolled their gardens, shouting their anguish at the sky and asking God why the Church had been abandoned to a bunch of liberal decadents. That of course was all before Karol Wojtyla took the rudder and steered the Bark of

181

Peter backwards into the secure waters of religious and theological certainty.

The dead priest had a big old nineteenth-century parochial house and he used to have parties where clerics and schoolteachers and members of the choir got so drunk that they fell about in the rose bushes on their way back to their cars to drive home in the dawn light.

The dead priest had been an inspiration to us in 1975. He was in his thirties then and he read the *New York Review of Books* and often brought us to Dublin to see Beckett's plays.

But when the Polish pope and the German theologian took over the Vatican, he just put his head down for thirty more years like many other liberals who were caught inside the organisation. Privately, they threw their eyes to heaven, sucked in the smoke of a thousand Marlboro cigarettes and worked their way through the single malts. What could they do? They were trapped. The people who might have been significant players in a liberal Church were sidelined and terrified into silence. I remember one professor who drank so much that he would occasionally be found sleeping on the doormat outside his own rooms – and Lunny drank so much that when he put his head down on the banquet table at a wedding in the parish nobody around the white table of coffee cups and dessert bowls noticed that he was dead until the groom was finished speaking and the best man called for Father to say grace.

'That was a lonely way to go,' I said on the phone to Enda, 'but the truth is I didn't like Fr Lunny. What did he do in the face of the catastrophe that has afflicted the Catholic Church during this past thirty years? He just became a drunk.'

There was silence for a few moments.

'I'm astonished,' Enda said, his voice a whispered cocktail of indignation and anger. 'I'm astonished you would speak so ill of the dead.'

'I'm not speaking ill of him,' I said. 'I'm just saying the truth. In fact, I feel sorry for him. But I won't be going to his funeral. I'm up to my eyes with work. Trying to get stuff written. And the wife is away and the roof is leaking. I'm just too busy.'

'Well,' he said, 'I thought you might just like to know.'

'But call if you're passing this way sometime,' I added. 'Love to see you. How's the wife?'

As if I cared. I had done the damage. I had committed an act of treachery against someone who had once been of great help to me. Sustained me intellectually and encouraged me to take risks.

'Separated,' he said tersely. 'Ten years. She wasn't well. Anyway, maybe I'll call sometime.'

'Do that,' I said, and hung up.

I made more coffee and sat staring at the ceiling. I wanted to see how bad the leak was. When nothing dripped, and I was fairly certain that the ceiling in the sun room wasn't

183

in imminent danger of collapse, I went off to my studio to meditate.

But it was difficult because I was still troubled by the dead priest, and the leaking roof that might be overcome later by further storms. And, besides, through the door I could see that the wind had scattered my five little stones all across the patio. So there I was sitting in the zen position, a cushion between my ankles and buttocks, my eyes half closed, the candle flickering on a table in the corner and the more I tried to relax, the more my mind filled with anxiety as I wandered in a fog of lament for my mother.

When I was nine months old, my mother decided that she had had enough. So a nurse was engaged. A teenager of exquisite beauty and tenderness who would steal me up a little bit of bread at night, to the back bedroom where my mother had abandoned me. I loved this nurse. I learned from her the music of the Cavan drumlins, the certainty of love, the pleasure of milk. But then at four years of age, the nurse vanished. She was let go. And there's not much you can say to a four-year-old after that. They don't understand how you can 'let someone go'.

As a result, I grew up with an uneasy suspicion that the mundane world was never quite dependable, and that the people around me were not quite reliable. And my mother, who had her own problems, appeared as an enigma to my eyes, a colossus that stared down at the baby on the floor wondering what she'd do with it, and me on the floor looking up at her, wondering who the fuck she was.

I comforted myself with vague memories of the beautiful woman I had lost, who used to feed me lumps of bread and who then vanished without explanation, and I always blamed her absence for the fact that by seven years of age, I couldn't knot my tie, belt my trousers or tie my shoelaces.

Looking back, it could fairly be said that I ought to have worked harder in school. And it's a pity I didn't play more with other children, trust them or talk to them; maybe even play a little football now and again. That's what children are supposed to do. Work as a team. And study. If I had even done a bit of homework every night, I might have got a good Leaving Certificate. Who knows, I might have become a doctor or an astronaut. But no, I was trouble from the word go – not to others, but to myself, a solitary child, a loner in the schoolyard, an infant abandoned by the queen of heaven. And then in adolescence, like all the other boys in my class, sperm flowed from my loins at night with the usual insistence of nature. But it terrified me. I feared that this was not a natural substance of my own making. This was the Godly essence of humankind. As if buckets of tiny unborn babies, lost souls, potential football teams were dying before they were born and every night I was bandaged more in wads of guilt and grief.

And to compensate for this concupiscence, as the priest in the confessional called it, I leaned a lot on Dominic

Savio, a watery saint who had died when he was about fifteen. I had a poster of him in my room. O her teenagers had Mao Tse-tung on the wall, a big fat smiling demon who was slaughtering all before him in China at the time and who was very fashionable among students in the Western world. The Mao poster was a way of saying to your mother that you were finished with her. The knot was broken. The umbilical cord had been severed in the teeth of Mao's sleazy grin and in the deep red stain of the poster – like the ocean of blood in which Mao was drowning his nation.

But Mao and his lusty revolution were not for me. No. I was committed heart and soul, on my bare knees, to a watery saint that no mother would want her boy-child praying to. And yet this jaundiced little creature in love with death was, for me, a more subversive role model than the chairman of the Chinese Communist Party, because his deep self-denial and his disengagement with the mundane world offered a sorrowful child like me an alternative reality. At night, Dominic induced in me dreams of death, and the life beyond death and the possibility of being enfolded once again in the arms of a beautiful woman who I lost so abruptly at the age of four. Religious fervour is what put me to sleep at night. That was, of course, after I had released into the cold universe another thousand unwanted souls spurting from the tip of my penis.

And then, instead of maturing in late adolescence by reading Camus and Sartre and realising that we all are alone in the universe, I tried to hold my divine mother's hand through life, trusting that she would always lead me home.

Except that, eventually, I let go. Because there is a kind of self-awareness in late middle age that rises up out of the loins, when the loins are old. It is a slow realisation that religious faith is just a therapy for depression, a way of masking one's anxiety about impending death.

And then finally in my fifties, I was obliged to confront my real mother again. Mammy, my very earthly mother, was now an ageing and infirm old lady, beginning to wobble and shake and eat Panadol like jelly babies and complain irrationally about the neighbours.

Eventually she died. My dear mother, after doing her best and getting nothing but a lifetime of disappointment from me, at ninety-six years of age took her last few breaths with intense concentration and serenity and in the passing of a moment, she was gone. The room emptied. The bones in the bed maintained no further significance beyond all the other dust in the universe. Mammy would not be there to hold me ever again.

187

And I'm not blaming her for anything. I couldn't. She was a great lady. A character. She was a small bird of a woman, agile in her mid-nineties and quick-witted. She could laugh and joke in company. She had a powerful turn of phrase. She played golf. She was an extraordinary cook. She relished having visitors to the house when we were young because she could relive again the days when she was a young woman walking the corridors of the Metropole Hotel in Cork, greeting guests, and ensuring that their linen was impeccable and that everything else in the room was to their satisfaction. She could hold her memories and live them again in brief affected exchanges with the occasional visitors who called to her in old age.

She loved Fred Astaire and Ginger Rogers and she danced with a coy feminine delicacy, but on the other hand, she was abrasively truthful. She could cut the socks off anyone who disagreed with her and, as she grew older, she engaged with doctors, bureaucrats and civil servants as if they were the enemy. Even as a widow, a bereaved queen in muted grey, her eyes could reach across a crowded dining room and connect with someone in the far corner, just to share her grief.

I remember nights when she was exuberant. When she was funny and happy and drank whiskey, and told great stories and danced with strangers. Nights when she came for Christmas and couldn't be put to bed until the singing ended. And earlier, when she was younger, I would accompany her to the weddings and dance with her, and she'd say, 'Where did you learn to dance so well?'

I sensed that my father danced like a donkey and, as he got older, he withered fast. But as she got older, something deeper darkened her face. Something never discussed.

I didn't really understand her until she died. I never got the full picture. It was only when I went into her house after the funeral and looked into the cupboards and drawers that I found something – like the tracks of the animal or like the markings on a cave wall – that suggested someone had been there and tried to scrawl in private and unconsciously a little of what it was like for them to be human.

It was all there in her house, the photographs and scraps of paper, the notes and diaries and shopping lists from the past. From them, I could patch a person together. By touching things, and smelling things, and reading little one-line notes about what she had paid for face cream or bales of turf briquettes I became closer to her than I had ever been when she was alive. And I became more ashamed of the ways that I had let her down.

THE ROOF OF our cottage had been leaking for years. We noticed it each winter. The same brown stains would appear on the ceiling during November. But they never seemed urgent. The stains were tiny. Like freckles. We would look at them sometimes as we ate our toast and marmalade in the mornings with a sadness that writers and artists acquire as they get older and poorer and can only watch the deterioration of their homes with stoic humour. It's part of the package for an artist that success is merely the postponement of failure and eventually an old age of anonymity and frugal living awaits us all.

I remember the beloved going off to London for a week in October after my mother had died, and I sat in Arigna looking up at the ceiling and feeling sad but not alarmed at the spreading brown stains above. I wasn't alarmed because that winter I had other things to worry about.

Like the fact that my mother's house was still locked up, untouched and unloved since the day she had died. And if the roof came off that house during a storm, I wouldn't even know about it. That's where the leaks could destroy a building that was already decaying because fires had not been lit regularly, and the windows were never opened to ventilate the rooms. We were heading into another winter, and it didn't seem right to leave it like a mausoleum, with dust gathering on her clothes, and fungi creeping in behind the wallpaper, and the radiators turning the bedrooms into incubators for creepy crawly things as the snow fell outside on the abandoned garden. It was all just a waste of electricity. In fact, I was so worried the house would deteriorate further that I pleaded with the solicitor to do something with it. But he just turned it back on me.

'Perhaps you could get a team of cleaners to go in and scoop out all the rubbish,' he suggested one day on the phone as I was driving through Carrick-on-Shannon. 'It's simple. Just put everything in one big skip.'

191

I said, 'I can't just put all her private things in a skip and send it to the dump. I'd prefer to burn everything. How could I throw her bed into a skip?'

Mother hadn't even wanted to get that bed. She'd said it was squandering money. But the nurse insisted that we get a new one and so off I went to the furniture store. It just about squeezed into the jeep, though it scuffed the upholstery on the roof and possibly dinged the back door. But it had to be done. Because a good bed is essential. Years ago beds were revered; old people would say that 'so-and-so had taken to the bed', as if that was a final stage of enlightenment. There wasn't much talk of heaven as a hectic zone; rustic theology didn't entertain any hyperactive angels flapping around in choirs; afterlife to the Cavan man was a big sleep, a great snooze, a long doze till Christ returned on tiptoe, at the dawn of a new tomorrow. The grave was just another bed, and eternity was a silence undisturbed.

192   I was trying to park when the solicitor had phoned. There was a Traveller wedding on the steps of the church and the street was jammed with vans, and settled people were gawping at the bridesmaids in pink dresses. I couldn't take my eyes off the belly buttons and talk to the solicitor and drive, all at the same time.

'I'll call you back,' I said, and turned off the phone.

There's a way nomads carry their bodies that mesmerises me. Settled people show their wealth by building houses, but the wealth of nomads is carried on their shoulders or hangs from their ears or their wrists. And the enormous houses that settled people build and that pepper the Irish countryside seem crude and ostentatious compared to the grace of a woman walking down the steps of a church wearing her grandmother's gold ear-rings, and carrying in her demeanour all the pride of seven generations who have lived on the side of the road, with nothing to call property but the elegant meringue of white satin in which her virginity is packaged.

When I had parked the jeep, I phoned the solicitor again and told him I was sick. He didn't understand what I was talking about.

'I have a cold that won't go away,' I explained.

'And what can I do about that?' he wanted to know.

'I need to go to a chemist,' I said. 'Therefore I can't think about the house today. I'll call you tomorrow.' And I hung up abruptly.

'I'm congested at night,' I said to the chemist. 'I'm afraid it might be an infection.'

She said, 'Is the mucus green?'

I didn't know.

She said, 'You'd better see your doctor.'

I coughed later on the street, and examined the result in a tissue. It had that light-green luminosity which the Virgin Mary statue used to display in my childhood bedroom when it glowed in the dark. There was a time when luminous Virgins were all over the place, but not any more – though the pound shop had a lot of luminous fingernails in the same shade of green on sale for Halloween.

I stepped into the pound shop to buy a haircutting machine, because I was fed up with long hair. But the girl at the checkout made a joke. 'Don't make a mess of it,' she said, and that worried me because I always make a mess of everything when I'm alone, so I resisted the haircutting machine.

'I don't want it,' I said to the checkout girl, even though she had put it through the till.

'OK,' she said, smiling, like she was trying to be pleasant to a walrus. 'No problem.'

The solicitor's number was coming up on my phone. But I was back at the chemist's for paracetamol and I noticed pink hairbands for sale on a rack inside the door. They were very pink, but that didn't seem important until I tied up my hair and examined the result in the jeep's rear-view mirror five minutes later. And then the solicitor's number came up again so in a complete fit of frustration, I went to a barber and had my skull shaved down to a number two.

After that, I was standing in a queue in the post office, feeling like a prisoner with a shaved head and emptying tissues from my pockets into the wastebasket, when the solicitor phoned yet again. This time I answered it.

'What?'

'There's a letter of intent that needs to be signed,' he said. 'We need your instructions on how to proceed. Are you keeping the house? Or selling it?' He sounded a bit shirty, I thought.

So I said, 'Isn't there something very elegant about the Travellers' tradition of burning the trailer when someone dies?'

There was a pause.

'They don't just throw out the old beds,' I added. 'That would be disrespectful. So they burn everything in an elegant immolation of all memory.'

The pause got longer.

'You want to burn the house?'

'No,' I replied, 'I suppose I don't.'

'Well, what *will* you do?' he asked.

'That,' I replied, 'is a good question.'

But I just couldn't articulate for him how difficult it would be for me to clean the house or even walk in the door, never mind try sorting out what its long-term destiny might be. Even when she was in the nursing home, I only went to Cavan in winter to check that the heating was on and the place wasn't going to be ruined by leaking pipes. And that was never more than once a month. And I'd dash in and out in ten minutes.

I would use the back entrance because the damp had seized up the front door. I'd go through the Perspex sun room at the rear and I'd be assaulted by a stale fragrance of human senility on everything I touched.

The house was so resonant with the echoes of her broken

heart, the fragments of her personal history, the unspoken archive of her sorrow that I couldn't bear to touch it when she was still alive and now that she had died it offended me to think of anyone else disturbing it. It was all a shrine to her departed ghost. How could I give a solicitor the keys or instructions to sell it? How could I do anything with it? Like any child who has lost a parent, I wanted to run away from my mother's house and never open that door again, but I didn't want anyone else to open it either.

'So how are you now?' a lanky countryman with a peaked cap asked me in the post office queue.

'Not great,' I said.

'And what's bothering you?'

'The house in Cavan,' I confessed. 'My mother's house. I keep getting phone calls from the solicitor wanting to know what's to be done with it.'

'Well,' he said, 'you'll not sell it. Cos it's worth nothing in a recession. So I suppose you'll be holding on to it.'

'Yes,' I said, and I thought about that for a moment. 'Yes. That's a good way of putting it. I'll be holding on to it.'

THE MORNING I heard of the priest's death, I went to Bundoran because I was suffering from cabin fever and I needed to get away from the leaking roof. It was a forty-minute journey through the deep glens of Leitrim, and the rugged swell of the sea is dramatic in a winter storm. I drove up the coastline near Mullaghmore, where young people cruised in 4x4s with cameras stuck out the windows to capture the rolling barrels of waves.

I parked at the waterfront, where enormous ocean breakers threatened the buttress wall and thumped on the beach. I went to an off-licence and bought a bottle of Bushmills whiskey for later in the evening, and I left it back in the jeep. Then I sat on a bench, remote and aloof from the surfers who were daring the ocean, and I tried to figure out where time goes or what happens to the past when it is forgotten.

I walked back towards the centre of town and had eggs and sausages in a small café on the main street. All around me, young couples were devouring late breakfasts, as young ones do after sex. They were talking about the previous night's fun in some nightclub. There was a clock on the wall that showed New York time, and another one told Irish time, which was helpful because one couple at the next table were so absorbed in each other's eyelashes that I doubt if they knew what continent they were on, never mind what time it was. The woman's face was transfixed, as if she were drowning in desire. As if she might just rip off her partner's shirt at any moment were it not for the proximity of other customers. As if they might slip into the toilet all of a sudden and get it all done in five minutes over the wash hand-basin.

I suppose it's encouraging to see young people filled with so much mutual desire that they don't notice anyone else in the room. As a young man, I was always amazed at how much exquisite anonymity could be found in the sexual act. And even in places like Maynooth, where a university campus was situated in the middle of a Catholic seminary, there were always dark corners, like the Student Union bar, and Saturday-night cider parties in the housing estates where the lay students lived, where if two strangers of the opposite sex were alone in a room for more than five minutes, they felt a moral obligation to try and ride each other.

And try they did, though few succeeded beyond a fumble in the dark or sleeping together with their underpants on. And the clerical students certainly didn't make love in many toilets over wash-hand basins like in the movies as far as I remember because they were studying for the priesthood. But my friend, the dead priest, was academic, erudite and burdened with a brilliant mind, and he seemed to understand the sexual revolution in a way that we didn't. He was modern; he had a car and money and he was already ordained. What did we know of his wide experience?

And I was just trying to be a poet. Not an easy thing either because, back then, poets were always serious men. Women sat beside them in silent adoration, or so the poets thought, as they smoked pipes and blathered in posh accents. I too sat at the feet of a few afflicted poets in Grogan's and other Dublin pubs, listening attentively, and almost doting on their slim volumes of poetry that lay on the tables between the pints.

But of course the women were not doting. They were just waiting for their time to arrive. Waiting for new voices in the public world. Waiting for Marian Finucane and other women to break the mould of the officious baritones on Irish radio. Waiting too for Maya Angelou and Sharon Olds and Sinead O'Connor and a legion of other poets and singers to spin the hurt and wound of their oppression, and weave new love songs and laments. In that patriarchal world of Maynooth, we hadn't even thought about the female orgasm, never mind thought that such an event might require our attention.

But the world outmanoeuvred the priest and me. Ireland changed. The Catholic Church got morally cornered, its clerics disgraced and its teachings made absurd by the insistence of women to be heard. Divorce arrived and gay people's private lives were decriminalised and young people in small villages began using condoms. The clergy with their gun-dogs that once traipsed the hills of Leitrim in search of pheasants were all gone. And the priest in everyone had been dead a long time before anyone knew it.

200   As I grew older, a woman became my compass and anchor, the ground and completeness of my universe. The beloved steadied me, but now she was not in sight. She was not near the windy beach in Bundoran that morning. She was probably in Poland having a morning coffee, or eating muesli with bananas, or heading off to some gallery or exhibition. She certainly was not with me on the windswept edge of the Atlantic. The clouds came fast in from the ocean and the wind flung leaves and twigs across the windscreen all the way back through Glenade

and Manorhamilton. The ugly wind turbines reared their heads on the mountain ridges as I passed Drumkeerin and a hen harrier hovered between two turbines watching for prey. At least the turbines didn't seem to bother them. A hare crossed the road in front of me and I could see his bulging eyes reaching away from the jeep's wheel. Then dogs came through the air, their teeth bared, and their eyes on me too for a moment before heading further in pursuit of their prey.

I lit the stove in the studio in the afternoon. Dead rose branches knocked on the glass windowpane. Smoke billowed down the pipe and flooded the room. It's a north-easterly that comes down the chimney but the ladder was locked away in the artist's studio and I couldn't find the key, so I couldn't climb onto the roof to cover the top with a bucket, which is the only solution. Instead, I endured smoke billowing out through every vent in the stove until I felt like a kipper and was forced eventually to abandon the studio for the rest of the day.

IT FELT LIKE my beloved had been a long time gone and not a single word from her by phone or Skype or text. No doubt she was having a great time in some bohemian world of wild Polish painters, drinking vodka into the late hours and listening to Chopin on old LPs. Or perhaps she had lost her mind and gone wandering over the border into the Ukraine, unable to find her way back, unable to text me, or explain to the police who she was? I didn't know.

Somewhere down in Laois, the remains of the priest were lying in a casket at the foot of the sanctuary where he had said his mass for many years. I brought my bottle of Bushmills whiskey in from the jeep because I intended drinking a few shots later as a mark of respect.

And then, at about five o'clock, there was a knock on the front door. The shadows had already enveloped the spruces and the small copse of birch, alder and oak near the house. The beech trees still rustled with last year's leaves. The ground was soggy. The mist had fallen on the roof. The fire in the sitting room was blazing, but I wasn't expecting anyone.

The young woman spoke with a French accent. 'Ah am very disappointed weeth you,' she said when I opened the door.

She wore a long brown coat belted at her slim waist and the collar turned up against the wind. A black beret sat level on her head, its black rim crossing her forehead above her eyebrows and reminding me of paramilitary men who used to infest the borderlands years ago.

'*Pardonnez-moi*,' she said, intuiting my alarm and taking it off.

'I thought you were a member of the old IRA for a moment.'

Her brown hair was parted in the middle but when the beret came off it fuzzed out in a big mess on both sides of her face.

'Who are you?' I wondered.

'*Une amie du prêtre mort.* How you say? A friend of dee priest ooo eeez gone.'

'Ahhh.'

'*Puis-je entrer?*'

'Of course you can come in,' I said, more than delighted at the prospect of female company. I was practically on fire with the idea of a French woman in the house. She stood for a moment beneath the porch light, loosening her belt and opening the coat to reveal a black dress and ankle-high boots and a black jumper over her slim body. The wind was blowing the ivy leaf around the door and I beckoned her inside thinking how much she resembled some movie star from 1940.

We sat at the fire in the front room. I poured whiskey into Waterford cut-glass tumblers and we chatted about the storms, the high tides, her purple Citroën and how she had got lost on her way from Donegal, heading for the funeral and then realised she was only a few miles from where I lived. Eventually we came back to the subject of the dead priest.

'*Vous le connaissiez?*' she said. 'You knew him?'

'I did. A long time ago.'

'So. *Pourquoi* you will not be coming, how you say, *à l'enterrement?*'

'Because I don't like funerals. I don't believe all that stuff. I don't want to hear what they will make of him. Wrapping him up in sentimental nonsense about going to heaven and how he was such a devout priest. I can assure you he wasn't very devout when I knew him. But of course that was a long time ago. He may have changed.'

'And do you not have, what is it, *peur de la mort?*'

'Of course I am afraid of death. The abyss ahead of us all terrifies the shit out of me.'

'But you have no faith?'

'I'm confused,' I replied.

She was staring into the fire. The flames flickered on her round spectacles.

'So you are not a person who likes funerals. Because the abyss of death frightens you,' she said.

'Correct.'

'And your mother?'

'What about her?'

'Did she die well?'

'Yes,' I said. 'It was an event of exquisite beauty. She lived in the moment, drew her breath, lay back and withered, vanished, like a leaf falling from a tree. It was beautiful. And I'm so grateful that I was there and that she was spared the religious trimmings.'

'You are an angry man too,' she said. 'You are ... *un chien dans la douleur.*'

'I'm afraid I don't know what that means.'

'Like a dog in pain,' she said coldly.

'Who are you?' I wondered.

She smiled but didn't answer.

205

'I better go,' she said, 'before this gets ugly.'

'Please,' I said. 'One more drink.'

'Well … OK,' she said. 'I will have, as you Irish say, one for the road.'

And if it had not been such a stormy night, I might have seen her as quite normal, and not some ghost flung up like flotsam out of my own dark unconscious.

But I did drink a bottle of whiskey with her, whether she was real or imaginary, this mysterious woman, this busybody in her little black dress and ankle-high laced boots. She might have been going out clubbing for the night for all I knew. She might have been working in Bundoran in a hotel. She might even have been heading for the funeral on the morrow. Nothing surprises me about young people. They wander where they will in the middle of the night and they're not afraid to knock on anybody's door.

I did it myself when I was in my twenties. I went to an island off the coast to visit a famous writer of the time. To knock on his door and declare myself a writer too and sit at his feet and learn the trade. I got a ferry from the mainland. The ferryman was a big bronze ox of a man, so firm in his limbs that he could barely walk. But when he was at the tiller, and had flung loose the ropes, and the wind was battering his brown leather face, he seemed like a formidable specimen of heroic masculinity.

'Do you know any writers on the island?' I asked.

'I do,' he replied, and spat into the Atlantic.

'What do you think of them?' I continued.

I was wearing shorts, tennis shoes and a sleeveless green T-shirt. With long hair flowing either side of my face, I was already uneasy that he might think me too effeminate to have on his boat.

'There was a writer came to this island years ago,' he said, 'and he was here a few years and then he went away and he wrote a book about everybody.'

He paused.

'And he never came back.'

He paused again. Thinking to himself about this man.

'Mind you,' he said, 'if he ever appeared on the mainland and was looking for a ferry, I would certainly take him. But he would never reach the island.'

He looked out again across the swell and spat once more and I could feel him breathing like a bull as he ruminated on the offence the writer had caused by writing about people's privacy.

207

Then he turned his gaze at my scrawny body, peeled my clothes off with a disgusted forensic stare and enquired, 'What do you do yourself?'

'I'm a teacher,' I replied instantly.

So it wouldn't have been totally unreasonable to suppose that this young woman really landed on my doorstep on a wintry evening because she had read some of my work, knew where I lived and wanted to talk to me about Kierkegaard or the qualities of modern Irish literature. At least that's the kind of thing I'd like to believe. That's the kind of thing I might fantasise about. But it's not the kind of thing that ever happens.

The truth is that I had conjured her up. I had called the ghost of Simone Weil to keep me company because I felt guilty about dismissing the dead priest. And of course she bore an uncanny resemblance to that same Simone Weil whose photograph I sometimes used as a screensaver on my laptop. So there we were, with the evening hurtling along without either of us in control.

She held her Waterford whiskey glass beside her cheekbone, with her elbow on the side of the armchair, and sometimes she rubbed the cold cut glass against her cheek. Sometimes too she would take off the small spectacles and rub her eyes and then replace them, scrutinising me in that moment as if I might be about to vanish. Other than that, she showed no sign of tiredness and little emotion. It's strange the way women who appear in men's sexual fantasies are always perfect. Not that this was a sexual fantasy – Simone Weil and I were just good friends.

I looked intently at her as she looked at the fire.

'You don't by any chance want some food, Simone?' I wondered.

'No,' she said, 'I don't.'

'And you're not by any chance my mother?'

'No,' she said, cringing at the question, 'I'm not your mother.'

'Well, that's all clear,' I said.

It was that time of the night. And half the whiskey was gone; too late for her to leave and too late to continue trying to make serious conversation. So I insisted. It was the only safe thing to do.

'We must eat,' I declared.

'Are you thick?' she said. 'Ghosts don't eat.'

'You're not a ghost,' I replied.

'I'm your fantasy.'

'No. You're a messenger; that's what you are,' I said.

Nevertheless, we went to the kitchen. I found beers in the fridge. She sat on a high stool and I clattered around the worktop with various pots and pans.

'Do you know,' I said, 'that there is a difference between solitude and silence? Silence is OK, it exists as a deep space in the human heart. You can share silence with another person; it's the emptiness in an atom, it's like the benign core of everything. It's the space between the notes that makes the notes beautiful. But solitude on the other hand is a prison of one's own making. Solitude is having no one. And I have been falling into solitude. I have been locked in that solitude since my wife left. Not silence. No. I am here in solitude and have become so cold and treacherous that I needed someone to turn up. And so here you are. But now I'm worried that even you being here won't break the bond of my solitude. You're just part of me, and both of us are here together in some terribly lonely embrace.'

I was staring at her beautiful young body and she looked a bit uneasy.

'Forgive me,' I said. 'I get over-excited. Did you ever hear the mind described as an unruly elephant? Well, mine is an unruly horse. I have a treacherous horse. I mean a treacherous heart. It clings to people and places, and sometimes I mistake these attachments for happiness.'

She started looking at the clock on the wall.

'When I was depressed, I used to play the flute. That sustained me for years. And, more recently, I have been cooking. Which is why we are here in the kitchen. Because I'm going to do pancakes.'

'For God's sake don't do pancakes,' she said suddenly. 'Make an apple tart.'

'Why?'

'Apple tart is safer. If you do pancakes, you'll set the place on fire – and probably poison yourself.'

'OK.'

And so I made an apple tart for the beautiful young woman.

'For me, cooking is a way of mending the broken world,' I said. 'An alchemy that makes a little bit of the universe OK.'

'You are very drunk,' she said, after I had slapped a quick pastry together and wrapped it around a few chopped apples and flung it in the oven on a baking tray where the tart oozed apple juice while I leaned over the worktop and polished off every beer in the fridge.

210

Michael Harding

'I am brooding on my mother's death, Simone,' I confessed. 'I am lamenting. That's why I am so sour.' And she seemed to understand.

My mother went sour. 'I'll be carried out of here in a box,' she used to say defiantly about her house, as if being human meant remaining there to the bitter end. But she wasn't carried out in a box. She was wheeled out to a nursing home. And yet, in another sense, she never left. I might as well have tried to dig her out from under the floorboards, because her spirit was so embedded in the foundations, the walls and the ceilings that she couldn't be moved. And her shadow fell on every door handle and on the backs of the chairs and on every little ornament. And the sound of her hand was in the creaking doors, and the tick and tock of the switches from the hot press to the central heating.

And she said that she didn't know what would happen to the place when she was gone. As if it existed for her and was so entwined in her psychic presence that it might turn to dust or air when she passed away. As if it might crumble. As if her consciousness was holding the slates intact on the roof. She had scrubbed the floors so often. Washed and painted the bathroom walls so often, and changed the crockery in the dining room china cabinet so very, very often. And she had made new covers for the sofas, and wove eiderdowns, and hung pictures, and sewed lining into the velvet curtains. And in December every year she scoured the kitchen cupboards. There were sheepskin rugs on every floor that she had stretched on frames in the back yard and cleaned the guts and gristle off herself, with porous stone reddening her knuckles.

One day when I was a child, Granny had come to the house to watch the Vatican Council on the television. Granny had her knitting with her, and I took up the needles and was trying to pass a stitch from one needle to the other, and Granny said, 'Stop that!' There was thunder and lightning outside and she feared that the stainless steel needles might conduct electricity from the sky down into my fingers. At least that's what she told me. I knew that if lightning struck it was more likely to strike the television aerial and blow up the Vatican Council on the screen, but I said nothing. And I suspect the needles were plastic and that Granny was making it up. But she certainly ruined my chances to develop an interest in knitting. And maybe that too is what she was up to, because boys didn't knit many jumpers back then.

I remember in the nursing home one day, I noticed an old lady knitting, the way Granny used to, and she was keeping a close eye on Mother, so that I imagined she was a guardian angel, knitting a scarf to pass the time.

Then the old woman put down her needles and said to me that she had been up half the night. 'If I'm depressed or can't sleep,' she explained, 'I knit. It takes my mind off other things.'

'That's right,' Mother said, staring out the window.

Michael Harding

There was another woman in the nursing home who had a child's doll. And she hugged it day and night. And a stout and cheerful woman, who spent all her waking hours in a wheelchair, sang 'The Old Bog Road' at Mother's ninety-fifth birthday party. We had afternoon tea, and a cake, and a man played the accordion. And then all together we sang 'The Old Bog Road'.

I too am getting old now. Drifting into an uncertain future where I'll soon be lighting the fire with difficulty, like all those old men in my youth who used to sit in the corner of their kitchens, grunting every time they moved. Back then, old people wore black and passed the time rolling up newspapers into firelighters or dangling string in front of cats or minding grandchildren from falling into the fire. But then the Celtic Tiger arrived, and everyone got jobs, and money emptied all the houses. People became oppressed by mortgages and they couldn't stay at home and so the old folks went off to nursing homes where they could sit in the day room and dream, knit or hug their little dolls.

So eventually my mother died. At ninety-six. At long last. And I'd go to her house in Cavan during those months after the funeral and look out at the wilderness in the back garden; the white lilac tree growing sideways so that it was impossible to get to the clothesline, the ivy breaking through the galvanised roof as it squeezed the garage to death. The evergreen trees had grown high and scrawny and up through the electricity wires. The phone line was

213

broken and straggled through the grass from the post to the wall of the house. I asked myself, is that the way she would want it?

Like this?

No. She would never have tolerated a garden so wild. And yet she herself *was* wild. In my psyche, she had become a devouring wolf and her teeth still ripped the meat from my bones every night when I lay down to dream in the huge double bed where she first imagined me.

'You're crying,' Simone Weil said.

'Yes,' I said, 'because she banished me in some way that I can't quite understand. And I miss her.'

'Go easy on the whiskey,' she said. I had almost finished the bottle.

'She hunted me away from the fireplace, she flung me into the dark. And I crave to be held by her, or to be held by my eternal mother, by Christ's mother, or by some angel or demon mother. To be held by my beautiful perfect mother who used to come betimes in unexpected visitations, but who comes now no more.'

'You are, how you say, off the wall,' Simone exclaimed. 'You need to chill.'

She was boiling a kettle.

'What's that for?' I wondered.

'Coffee,' she said.

'Listen to me,' I said. 'Listen to me.'

And I think that's where everything went black. I lost

track of things. Simone Weil went away and I went to bed.

But I didn't sleep. In the middle of the night, I woke with a pain in my stomach and I went roaming the house to see what damage I had done. One cut-glass beaker was broken. Tea was spilled everywhere. The empty whiskey bottle was on the floor in the kitchen. The cat was finishing the last of the apple tart and I pushed her away, because I think it was the uncooked pastry that had ruined me. My belly felt tight and rock hard. My stomach was distended and my skin was on fire.

In the front room, the fire had gone out. There was a north wind rattling the ivy against the windowpane and the sky had opened to the stars. The house felt like a fridge but of course I was only wearing pyjama bottoms. I went to the bathroom to piss and I could sense my toes going numb on the tiles. I tried to scratch the side of my leg while I was urinating and then dribbled piss on my pyjama leg.

'For fuck's sake,' I roared in a rage, and I vowed to give up alcohol for ever.

I went back to the bedroom and lay awake, listening to the wind and waiting for the morning light.

When it came, my stomach was still sore, I had a headache and my cheeks were hot. I spent a few disturbing moments in the toilet, but by lunchtime I was well enough to go to the Gala store in Drumshanbo. I got a take-out stew and returned to the house, where I ate it in the kitchen like a child, with a soup spoon, and threw the apple tart in the bin.

Later that evening, Nellie Finlay arrived. Not an angel or a demon or a mystic philosopher in a black dress, and certainly not the misty-eyed mother of any Christ. Just Nellie, my mother, the visual memory of an ordinary woman. She rose up out of the floor with powerful intensity, a frail little lady, who had sat in that same kitchen years earlier, watching Christmas mass on the television, her lips moving silently as the Pope of Rome intoned his blessing to the world.

I lit the fire in the front room. I got a blaze of coal roaring up the chimney and I turned on the television to watch another episode of *Girls*. But *Girls* was empty now. It was the chair across from me that gripped my attention. I stared at it, remembering her. A woman whose heart I had never quite reached. At least I could hold her there for a little longer, before every bit of her dissolved for ever.

I KNOW THAT there are no ghosts in the modern world – I suppose it may have been electric light that finished them off – but maybe there are angels. Because I did get a fright when I went to Cavan to stay in my mother's house not long after she had died.

It was All Soul's Eve. Maybe that's why I imagined I saw something. At first, it was just a queasy feeling. I just hadn't the stomach to go inside the house. It was late afternoon. The darkness was seeping out of the trees and the earth and enveloping the house, and the house looked bleak. I glanced at the upstairs windows and thought I saw someone standing there behind the curtain. Thought I saw the curtain move. I felt someone was looking at me. And then the curtain moved again and I was certain I saw a hand. I stood on the roadside looking at the dead windows, as inviting as empty eye sockets, and the grass growing on the roof, and the crows cawing from the chimney tops. It was the end of November. The evening was getting darker. *Perhaps things will look better in the morning*, I thought.

So I booked into a hotel in town and, the following day, I was out early. I found a small Gala shop with a café, close to the bus terminal beside the bridge, that served breakfast rolls to the early birds, though there were no queues now; no men in yellow jackets or work boots covered with yesterday's cement any more. The young woman behind the counter used to know them all by name, but she told me that they were probably all gone back to Poland since the economy collapsed.

I got talking to a slim girl in an anorak with a rucksack, sipping coffee by the window and toying with her scarf. Her father had left her to the bus station. She was a student at the College of Art and had missed the bus because she was combing her hair in the station washroom. So she decided to eat before heading off to hitch a lift.

'What bus did you miss?' I enquired.

'The Donegal–Dublin Express,' she said. 'It stops in Cavan.'

She didn't have to tell me that. When I was young I was familiar with all the buses in Cavan that went to Longford and Granard, and stopped in small towns like Crossdoney or Killeshandra, and at every laneway where some woman with a string shopping bag wanted to get off.

But one day in the yard of our primary school, an academy on a hill just above the bus station, the rumour went around that Cavan was getting 'an express'. I didn't know what 'an express' was. I thought it might be a press, like the things in the kitchen where Mammy hid the fig rolls.

'Oh, no,' a senior boy explained in the schoolyard. 'The express is a new type of bus. It's like a train. It doesn't stop anywhere and it will go all the way from Dublin to Donegal. In fact, the only place it *will* stop is Cavan, so that they can cool the engine and people can go to the toilet. It won't even stop in Navan,' he added gleefully. He was a real encyclopaedia.

In those days, there were still boys who wore dickie-bows and little grey suits at school to distinguish them from the lower classes. Nobody knew what an express looked like and we wondered why it would be called 'an express'. Once again, it was one of the posh boys who enlightened us.

'The express is not its name,' he said, sneering at us. 'In fact my daddy says it's going to be called the Cú-Uladh. It's named after Cú Chulainn's dog, who was quite a fast dog.' Smart boys were smart because they had parents who knew

219

interesting things and they always started sentences with phrases like, 'My daddy says …'

I was very proud of this bus to Dublin. It assured me that Cavan was on the world map and that I lived in a place of significance.

'It was called the Cú-Uladh,' I said to the girl with the scarf.

She had never heard it called that. But then she's from another generation. And it is unlikely that we would have spoken to each other at any other time of the day. She would be trapped in her own little world and I would be trapped in mine. A young woman and a middle-aged man is a poisonous cocktail, according to the ancestors. Though in the darkness before dawn, we were only shadows, and the other tables were occupied so the possibility arose for each of us to escape our restricted worlds and have a little chat.

220   'I've seen you before,' she said. 'Are you from Cavan?'

'Yes, I grew up on Farnham Road,' I explained.

The dregs of her coffee remained in a plastic cup on the table between us.

'I hate this time of year,' she said, hugging the cup with both hands, and gazing sideways out the window at a taxi man having an argument with a suitcase.

'And I hate waiting for buses,' she added. 'So I better head off and hitch.'

'I'm always waiting,' I said.

'What? For the bus?'

'No,' I said. 'For nothing in particular. I wait for letters a lot of the time. And I wait for the phone to ring. And I wait for good news that I always believe is just around the corner. In fact, one of the pleasures of being a writer,' I said, 'is that I get lots of time to wait.'

'You're up early,' she said. 'I thought writers lay in bed all day, with hangovers from the night before.'

I said, 'That's a tourist's idea of writers.' She was fidgeting again with the scarf around her neck.

'I better go,' she said.

But there was something sad about her. As if she was missing someone.

'The mornings are getting very dark,' she said, as she sighed and looked out the window. 'I don't like the dark.'

You can't tell nowadays if young people know anything about religion, so I didn't bother telling her that such mornings remind me of the days when I was an altar boy, my nostrils alert to candle wax and my belly rolling with hunger in anticipation of a good breakfast after mass. Days when old men and women shuffled into their pews or muttered prayers to the Virgin Mary on the side altar so loudly that all their anxieties rattled around the painted ceilings. That might have been too much information for a young woman in these secular times. So I asked her if she would like me 'to freshen her coffee', a phrase I first learned from waitresses in American diners.

If I had said, 'Do you want another coffee?', she might have said no. But the phrase made her smile. And then it dawned on me that she might not refuse a breakfast either.

'Can I treat you to a full Irish?' I wondered. 'It might help you if you're hitching.'

'Thanks,' she said. 'But really, I'm OK.'

'It's a very dark morning,' I persisted. 'Forecast says we might even have snow later.'

'OK,' she said, and smiled.

And when I returned with two breakfasts on a tray, she had taken out a book with 'Business Management' written on the front cover. I reminded myself of advice I once heard from a Japanese actor in Paris.

Only a young man should play the role of suitor. Older men ought to seek rewards by playing the wise uncle.

So I ate my sausage and pudding and spoke as softly and wisely as I could, declaring that a happy life sometimes depends on embracing the dark.

'Enjoy these short days!' I said. 'Enjoy the cold wind, and the flames in the fire, and the promise of snow!'

'Are you mad?' she asked, with the affection that only Cavan people can give that question.

'I'm from out the road,' I said, which explained everything.

Her eyes lit up and she said that there was one thing she

had loved about early mornings when she was a child.

'My mother used to make pancakes,' she said. 'I used to love that.'

'Does she not make them anymore?' I wondered.

'No,' she replied, very quietly. 'My mammy died when I was twelve.'

And she stared straight at me with a lovely gaze.

'You're sure you don't mind me sitting with you?' I said, for no particular reason.

'No,' she said. 'It's kind of nice.'

So we ate our breakfasts with relish then, two orphans in the November mist, and afterwards I paid the bill to the woman behind the counter who was already sliding layers of lasagne into the oven for the dinners later in the day. I dropped my companion at the road for Dublin where she might hitch a lift and I headed back to my mother's house.

THERE WAS A time when every Cavan woman was my mother. In the old days, Cavan women had a tendency to force-feed other humans. Perhaps it was due to poverty in the Drumlin region, a place of small farms and millions of chickens. There was a shadow of hunger and famine on the drumlins, which women compensated for by stuffing as much food into other people – particularly children – as they possibly could.

Or perhaps this compulsive behaviour in Cavan women was the effect of the Reformation, brought to the region by John Wesley, Presbyterians, and a variety of strict Christian sects, which repressed all urges of the flesh and created in Cavan people a tendency to express affection by way of verbal insults, accordion music and pinching each other on the bottom. In Catholic marriages, Cavan people's vanity was intensely policed by the clergy and this resulted in a society of plain hairdos, unvarnished nails and lips without rouge. When young adolescents in Cavan emerged from the time of the bottom-pinching, they found themselves in marriages where affection could only be legitimately expressed with large plates of bacon and cabbage.

Or perhaps the condition is endemic across the nation. Perhaps all Irish people live unconsciously within the force field of the eternal mother, the great Mammy.

For instance, Glangevlin in west Cavan is intrinsically linked with the Myth of the Green Cow of Gevlin who provided milk for all Ireland every day, until a witch came to her owner and said, 'I bet I can find a vessel that the cow will not fill.'

The witch took out a sieve and placed it beneath the cow. 'Try that,' she said.

They milked the cow for three days and nights until she bolted across the hills, her udder dragging behind and creating a gap in the Cuilcagh Mountains. And the cult of the great Mother endures. Young women in petrol stations and Gala shops and Centra cafés all around the country feed dinners to large, rugged truck drivers every day, in the name of the great Mammy.

It's something I can't avoid when I'm travelling in the jeep, from Kenmare to Belfast, or from Letterkenny to Ballycotton, in and out of Birr, Athlone and other midland towns as I round the roundabouts and zigzag up and down the country when I'm doing readings, giving talks, telling stories and generally acting the cod for a living. Everywhere I see the same thing – grown men standing in queues, like little boys, as some young woman from Kraków or Gdańsk feeds them braised steak and asks them do they want gravy on their spuds. The great Mammy incarnates and is made manifest in a thousand different women behind the nation's counters every day, all aproned for business; a vestment that can transform anyone into Mammy. A woman may be from Lithuania or Russia, or she may be only sixteen years old, but once she dons the apron she assumes matriarchal authority, and every middle-aged man on the road waits in line with the excitement of a ten-year-old child.

Coffee, walnut and chocolate cakes, apple tarts, vanilla cheesecakes and banoffee pie. And soups. And ovens of roast pork, bacon or beef, and garlic potatoes. Teachers phone in their orders. Students queue and swarm around the hot pots, and old men from the hills, who have lived alone since their wives died and who can no longer bear to cook alone. Meals go out the highways and byways of rural Ireland six days a week, tens of thousands of dinners every day, and even more on Wednesdays when the local papers appear in the shops.

I used to bring my own mother to such a food counter in Cavan every Friday, for many years, and we'd take the food back to her kitchen and eat it.

'Isn't this wonderful?' she'd say.

And I'd say, 'Yes, Mammy.'

And she'd say, 'Sure, you couldn't cook as good as this.'

And I'd say, 'No, Mammy, I couldn't.'

And I can't. Which is why, when I was staying in Cavan after her death, I went back to the same café every day at lunchtime for dinner, and often purchased an extra soup or a breast of chicken as well for my evening meal. I slept in the back room and spent the days sitting on the chair my mother had sat on and staring out the window at the cathedral spire in the distance, the hill of young ash trees and the copper beeches in a neighbour's garden, wondering all the while what my mother had been thinking about as she had watched that view for almost forty years.

227

A week later I was still in Cavan. The girls that forecast the weather on the television were promising snow. I played Chopin in my earphones and a pallid light folded the streets in ambiguity as if the world were dead. The trees were bare. The same old radio programmes persisted. The same old politics. The same old economy. Even the garden was dead. And it was the same old garden in which I had caught bees as a child. Even the young children on the streets going to school were the same – just another wave, another generation, another cluster of cuddly boys and girls in uniforms who think that their moment in time is unique.

I went to Dunnes Stores and the post office and various places that I used to frequent with her when she was still mobile. We used to go to Bridge Street and I would tell the staff in the Roma Restaurant that they had the best chips in the world, and I'd get two bags and two fish and I'd explain to them that my mother was outside in the jeep.

She would sit in the passenger seat, eating the hot, salty potatoes from a brown bag, relishing them, chip by chip. And relishing the view from the jeep. The same Bridge Street where she had grown up, minded her little brother Oliver and chased a cat.

But now I went to the chip shop alone and asked for a single bag. And they said nothing. I returned to the jeep beside the river, and stared out at the empty car park hoping for snow. Not that it snowed much that winter. It was mostly cold and wet.

I did see snow once. It was on a Thursday afternoon, and I had already seen the cold, blue flame in the fire the night before.

The first of it fell from a grey sky, a low cloud in the winter light. There was a luminosity in which a single flake fell and then another; one at a time, one every twenty minutes as I stood at the front door of her house. I imagined a soul flying upwards to another life as each flake fell down and each single flake was the crust that those departing souls left behind. Then the big snowflakes arrived. Unexpected. Like love letters. And they whispered when they met the grass on the lawn. Each flake singularly. It was almost possible to hear their promises as they met the blades of grass. And then the real snow came in the dark. Whorls like salt that flew around in wind pools. Then came the snow that fell when I was sleeping and covered the roads and ditches, folding them into a silent, crinkled wonderland that, in the morning, bounced so much light onto the ceiling of my bedroom that I woke as happy as if Mammy had returned from town in a big blanket. But it didn't last. By lunchtime, it had dissolved to slush. The rain fell. I cleaned out the ashes, and drove into town to comfort myself with another hot dinner from the Gala café.

But Glenasmole wasn't going to dissolve any time soon. That house was made of bricks and mortar. It existed on paper, in folios, and I hoped that the probate would soon be completed and the titles changed and I would become the new owner and she would fade from it forever.

That house must have been the crowning glory of her young life. And like many semi-detached houses in suburbia where women pottered about in 1950, it was a lonely little castle, into which she accommodated herself with stoic silence. And she never got tired of it. Although when she was seventy, after a decade of widowhood, she began going on foreign trips. Sick of her lonely fireside, she began travelling with Active Age groups to Brussels and Copenhagen and the Aran Islands, where she took photos that nobody ever looked at only herself and that were still in the drawers in the front room when I opened them; moments on piers or in restaurants or standing outside famous churches with widows from all over Europe.

By her eighties, she had reached a state of equanimity. There was no more travelling and no more pretending. She sold the car and there was no escape from what lay ahead.

She would look around the front room while I was sitting with her, and Alex Higgins was still alive and potting all the blacks, and she'd say, 'What will become of this place when I'm gone, this glen of thrushes?'

And she could still wash her own clothes when she was eighty-five. I remember seeing her in the kitchen on a stool, staring at the clothes tumbling in the machine, as if she was watching television, the unresolved grief for her husband's death still lingering. And she ate out of a saucepan, the same soup for four days.

'I've no one to cook for anymore,' she said one day, when I opened the fridge and found it cluttered with mouldy sausages. She lived on bowls of porridge from the microwave.

But she'd seemed content in the nursing home, her eyes closed as she dozed in the day room, and I wondered what she might be dreaming of; a time before telephones or emails perhaps, when lovers wrote their sweet nothings in letters that were transported across the countryside by horse-drawn coaches. A dream with no soundtrack, except perhaps for the clanging hammer of a blacksmith sweating over his fires, making wheels for carts and shoes for horses that pulled heavy loads on the stony highways.

That's the wondering that rose in me each time I walked in, and saw her dozing, at peace after all the wars that she had waged in Glenasmole when she was alone and angry and the only way to express it was by throwing the walking aid at whoever turned up.

She was reared at a time when the clop of a horse was the only noise on the streets, and traffic was the sight of a thousand horses gathered on a fair green.

One day, I said to an old man in the day room that it must have been pleasant back then, without the noise of televisions.

231

'No,' he said, 'it wasn't pleasant at all. In the 1950s, you could meet three or four grown men in any farmyard, as idle as infants, all gawking out of hay barns or cow byres, or standing against the gable wall of the house like imbeciles.'

'Why was that?' I wondered.

'All on account of the mammy,' he said. 'People were very poor, but the mammy would be too proud to let her sons go out and work as labourers. She'd keep them at home until they were destroyed.'

Not that there's anything wrong with pride. We're all proud until we grow old and find ourselves holding the wall for support, or foraging in Marks and Spencer for long johns, and trousers with elastic in the waist, like the ones I bought for her every so often.

'Your mother sleeps well,' the old woman with the knitting said. And the old man nodded. They knew her, even when she no longer knew herself. They sheltered her there in the day room and the woman with the doll reached out one day and offered it to her, as if Mother might like to play with it. But Mother refused. Her refuge was a handbag, which she clutched in both hands.

'Our Lady appeared in the trees when I was young,' a woman told me one day. 'Two girls were going up for milk to the big house when they saw her along the avenue in the tallest trees. And it went on for a long time and it was a huge sensation. And people would be ferried out from Mullingar on the back of lorries every evening. And there was a young lad who used to climb up into the trees, and he'd be making a joke of it all, shouting, "She's coming!" But one evening didn't he fall out of the tree and break his leg. So that put a stop to his gallop. And there was another man who made a business from the apparition. He cut branches off the trees along the avenue and sold them. And he made a fortune out of those twigs, even though they weren't even from the right tree.'

Mother sighed again.

The other woman said, 'Your mammy is definitely not in good form today.'

And it was hard to believe that maybe she was finally coming to the end of her road, because I still remembered all those lunches in the Kilmore Hotel, as if they were only yesterday, when my daughter was still in a high chair throwing spaghetti at the walls, and Mother would cast her eye around the dining room as we entered, and clutch her stick, to see if there was anyone there she knew.

'Hello, Nellie,' they'd say, and she would light up, and it felt lovely to be out with her for the day.

And I still remembered all those Fridays, as if they were only last week, when I would bring her into town to do the messages because, even in her late eighties, she still wanted to do everything herself. She'd totter around Dunnes Stores holding on to me or her walking stick or leaning against an aisle of biscuits or holding the elbow of any member of staff who was near, and she'd check the sausages, yoghurts, sliced pans and cold hams with a sharp eye. She was so particular. And at the checkout, she'd go through each price with the girl on the till and then erupt.

'Oh, that's far too expensive,' she'd say to me. 'Put it back on the shelf and get me the yellow one,' by which she meant a cheaper brand.

And the people in the queue waited. I longed for someone to throw a tantrum or fling a wire basket at her. But they didn't. They smiled and waited while I went to fetch a cheaper brand and when I returned feeling ashamed and foolish, she'd speak loudly, saying, 'What kept you?'

Then she'd turn to the audience and say, 'Sure, he's useless.' A tiny smile on her mouth as she became empowered by disempowering me.

She had a walking stick that she pointed at other people. I remember a particularly devout little lady who never ceased doing works of kindness for other Christians and who came to visit Mother regularly, in case she needed anything, or just to talk and cheer her up beside the electric heater in the front room.

But Mother didn't like her. She had resigned herself to solitude and she was content in the privacy of her own sour space. That's the fearful thing about depression. It's an isolating experience. It's a merciless solitude, like a glass wall surrounding the victim, leaving them alone, even in a noisy street, drenched with their own delusions and tormented by their own personal demons.

One day, she announced to me over the phone that the pious little lady had stolen the bed linen out of the hot press. So the next time she called, Mother demanded the linen back, and then slammed the door in her face. And she never spoke to her again after that. She even went to the guards to tell them of the crime. They smiled to themselves and said that there was nothing they could do and that was an end to it. Except occasionally when I was helping her from the jeep across the underground car park to the lift in Dunnes, she would recognise the woman in the distance and sometimes she would raise her stick and say, 'Look! That's the faggot who stole the linen.'

The time I spent in Glenasmole after she died was a necessary ritual of cleansing and dismantling her world, of taking her identity apart, of disposing of her wardrobe, so that the painters and decorators and carpenters could move in and construct something new. I longed for a time when I would no longer hear her voice whispering at the turn of the stairs, her muffled cough in the dead of night or her hand on a door as she slipped from room to room. I even wanted to replace all the doors in the house so that in the opening and closing of them, I would no longer hear her hand fall. That's why I went to stay at Farnham Road that November. She was four months dead and a job was waiting to be done. The nettle had to be grasped.

And then one evening in late November, I went to Mullingar to visit friends. He is Irish and she is from China. She cooked dumplings and stir-fried some vegetables and sliced up some raw carrots and we all tucked in. I called her Little Lotus for fun. She was a young woman who had been reared as an only child by elderly parents in the hills of a remote region in China. In the mornings, her father would do tai chi on the wooden balcony outside the house while his wife pottered about inside making tea and trying to remember where she left her knitting or trying to find her glasses. She could never remember where her glasses were, and she needed them to find the chickens, though the strange thing was that she didn't need them to knit. And she needed them to see her husband, who was much bigger than a chicken, but she didn't need them to thread a needle.

How the family ended up in a small wooden house with a balcony on the slopes of the hill beside a deep river is something their daughter never asked, in all the years that she went to the school in the local village or even when she went away to secondary school in a far-off town. Home was always home. Until she finished school and realised she must go to the city to find work.

When she was a child, her father, who even then was old and as slender as a single bone, would often take the horse and cart down the dusty lane to the village, where he drank more tea and talked to other old men, and then the horse would take him home.

236   In the warm afternoons, he liked to doze in the cart as it trundled up the stony laneway that reminded him of his childhood, and the horse was a reliable navigator because there was always oats at home.

It was the same nag that brought his daughter to the local bus station when she was leaving for Europe. Her father was waiting in the cart and she was standing on the balcony, in a bright flower-patterned dress and bare shoulders, and he said, 'Young girls are not fond of drapery at the best of times but you must wear a cardigan when you get on the bus, because it is six hours to the city and you will get cold when the sun goes down.'

So she went back into the house and lifted a navy blue cardigan from the chair and her mother looked up from her book wondering for a moment had the universe conspired to stop her daughter from emigrating.

'I thought you were gone,' her mother said, full of sudden hope.

'I just came back for this,' the daughter replied, picking up the blue cardigan, and in that moment her mother spoke her name and gave her a final hug.

There is a hug that happens after all the hugs, which is more valuable than gold. It is the extra hug. It is the hug that happens when someone is leaving, when the goodbyes have been said, and the fussing over luggage has been done twice over, and when the tears have been avoided and the manly coherent hugs have all been delivered and the emigrant is about to step away and become a ghost for ever. And then something is remembered. The keys. A passport. Or a cardigan. And at that last moment, the one who is about to leave turns again and says, 'I forgot something,' and suddenly there is time for one last, enormous hug; that extra hug that a child can carry with them across the mountains and over the ocean.

It's what I longed for from my mother. But which she could not offer. She burned with love for her children, but she failed us. And the pity is that I failed her too. I could have hugged her. I could have made myself a father to her child and made her warm and safe in her old age but in that I failed terribly. So we circled one another. And like the oyster in pain who wraps time around the sand and grows a pearl, so she weaved her widowhood in solitude around small regrets until she had become aloof and dignified in her sorrow.

The morning after I heard Little Lotus speak of her mother's hug, I walked into town, past lawns that in summer time had been drenched with flowering hydrangea, fuchsia, variegated ivies and big juicy red rose bushes. Now they were all dead. Bare branches and wrinkled rosehips stood in the winter fog. The laurel and the box hedges had been clipped back to smooth and severe lines. Clearly the middle classes had not been idle during the autumn. The cut lawns of Farnham Road glistened in a film of dew and the air was crisp.

In Dunnes Stores, I went around the familiar aisles and filled my shopping basket with all her favourite groceries, which I knew by heart. I bought a packet of Barry's tea, and six Activia yoghurts, and two slices of Brady's ham, and a half-loaf of bread. I bought cheese slices and half a dozen sausages. And for myself, I bought a Danish pastry and a bar of soap and three bottles of bath salts and oils, and at the checkout there was yet one more old lady ahead of me in the queue, counting her change. She had a wine-red beret on her white head, and was suspicious that the checkout girl might have cheated her. Everyone waited patiently. There was no telling how great were the things she had lost in a lifetime, or what was in her heart, but she got no satisfaction from the checkout girl before she walked away muttering something about life not being fair.

I walked home again, past the bus and the train stations and past McCarron's bacon factory where Nellie Finlay's father had sold his pigs. He would buy the pigs in Belfast, and convey them by train to Cavan. Mr Dolan, the old man at my mother's funeral, told me about him and how a crowd of young boys would gather at the station wall as the train pulled in, everyone hoping big John Finlay was on board, and that they might earn a few pennies by driving the pigs from the station down the hill to the factory.

In my own childhood, the factory owner, Tom McCarron, a remote patriarch with watchful eyes, had a Jaguar car that floated silently down Farnham Road and bounced up on the pavement outside the factory like a big boat coming to rest on a beach. I would finger the chrome cat on the bonnet as I walked home from school and listen to the squeal of pigs inside the factory, as they were shuttled along cables upside down to their awful death. I could not imagine what was in their hearts, but I certainly deduced that for some unfortunate creatures life was never fair.

That evening I cleaned out the bath. There was a seat in it for an invalid, whereby the care worker could wash my mother in the years when she was still able to climb upstairs. And all around the floor, there was dust and old wallpaper and flecks of peeling paint from the ceiling where the pipe had burst in 1996. I cleaned the bath and took musty towels from under the sink and threw them in the washing machine. I turned on the immersion heater downstairs and after a few hours, I poured half a bottle of bath salts into the steam. I lit incense sticks on the corridor and on the window ledge and in the bedroom. And then I undressed and got into the bath. I was ten years old again, a time when my body was small and fragile, and I longed to be a grown up. I soaked for half an hour and got out and dried and lay on the bed and fell asleep.

The next night, I did it again. I used more bath salts and soaked again, this time with night lights burning in the bathroom and on the ledges of the windows, and more incense sticks burning throughout the house. I set them on every window sill, and in jam pots on the corridor and on the mantelpiece in the back bedroom. Everywhere, except the front bedroom. I didn't go in there at night.

Only in daylight did I open that door and go through her stuff systematically. I put away the linen, the clothes, the suits, the frocks, all in different bags. Some went to the waste disposal and some to charity shops. And one day, I was packing away a drawer of lingerie and night clothes and I found presents from long ago Christmases, unopened gifts she had received and purchases she had made, still in cellophane wrappers with the price tags on the side in old pounds and shillings and Christmas cards still in their envelopes. I found a blue nightdress in a dusty presentation box, unopened since the 1960s, and I took it from the box and shook it free from the cellophane wrapping. It was a coy thing that some young girl might have worn back then with a lot of lace trimming on the hem. A present perhaps from someone who hadn't noticed the passing years; hadn't realised that Mother was by then almost fifty. And perhaps that's why it remained unopened. She may have felt herself too old for it. A light-blue, knee-length garment with short sleeves, lace ruffles on the shoulders and ribbons tightening the bodice and tiny roses in dark purple woven into the hemline. I brought it upstairs and left it lying on the duvet in the bedroom and stared at it for a long while.

Each afternoon, I would go to a charity shop on Bridge Street with another armful of dresses and frocks and cardigans and conservative suits in tweed and wool. The daily bundles were small because each time they were sorted I would change my mind. I would put half the stuff back in the wardrobe, convincing myself that some items were too valuable to let go. *They might be designer stuff*, I argued. *I might find some use for them. Perhaps my wife or daughter would like to have a look at them.*

But I forced myself to fill one bag each day until eventually the wardrobes and drawers were empty. Then at night, I lit the fire and the candles and put on the immersion heater and switched on her old transistor radio to hear concerts from the Wigmore Hall and Budapest on BBC3. And at bedtime, the landing upstairs grew dense with incense and I went to the bathroom and soaked and softened and wept. And afterwards I lay on the bed and covered myself with the sheets and fell asleep, holding the blue nightdress in my arms. And one night I pulled myself into it and let it hang around my body, and lay there feeling its delicate texture all around me, and then sleeping felt like drowning in the place where she first imagined me.

BUT YES, MAMMY, I was soft, and I am soft, and sentimental. And I've always believed in heaven. Ever since I was six and decided to climb trees instead of watching the *Lone Ranger*, which is when the Virgin Mary first appeared to me and enveloped me in her tenderness. I had gone up the main trunk of a chestnut tree, and sat on its lateral branches all afternoon, thinking myself equal to a monkey, when Desmond, my best friend, started pretending he was another monkey at the base of the tree. There was a dead spruce lying against the beech, which afforded me a path of escape as the other monkey came up the tree towards me. But the spruce was rotten and, as I scampered down, the branches gave way beneath me, like the shells of a thousand eggs, and I fell on my head and damaged my back. I lay on the floor of the wood, in awe of gravity, and terrified of you, because you weren't soft, Mother, especially when we made mistakes. I knew you would scold me severely for climbing trees. But that thought was swiftly replaced by serenity as I looked at the sky. I think it was the branches whipping my back as I fell that put eggshells in my mind, and the blue of the sky that suggested the Queen of Heaven. My back may have been lacerated by the branches, but, inside, I felt like a bird fallen from its nest, and was certain that Mother would come soon – not scolding, but rather enfolding me in her arms, and reassuring me that I was OK. I didn't see anything as literal as the porcelain Virgin commonly associated with Catholic apparitions in my moment of ecstasy; it was more a vague feeling of security. Later in life, my therapist explained to me that it was my own unconscious that fabricated a heavenly mother in the blue sky. The point is that it wasn't you, Mother, who held me then. It wasn't you.

And of course, it wasn't just you who was growing old. It was also Oliver, your little brother, now alone, playing the piano and reading old record reviews he had cut from newspapers decades earlier, and dozing by the fire, until tiny cancers finally crept up on him and devoured all his music.

And it was all the other folks in Cavan who you grew up with; the school friends, shop boys, chicken farmers, dressmakers, dancers, singers and hackney drivers, and the young girl friends with whom you shared secrets when they were having their babies; all those mothers walking the roads with prams four deep, proud as punch and not worried about oncoming traffic – they had all turned grey or were already gone before you to Killygarry graveyard.

All over Ireland your generation was fading away; their histories were fading, the buildings they were familiar with, the geography of where they were born, and their own passions and memories, obsessions and fears, their views on world wars or communism or long hair or apparitions of the Virgin Mary; everything that held them was fading into a kind of grey dust.

One generation always gives way to the next. Young people make noise and have the parties and claim the space.

Carpe Diem!

Old people shrink, retreat and dissolve into the bland paintwork of a doctor's waiting room. And now I see myself dissolving, because I am next in line and young ones are already dancing in spaces where soon I too will not belong.

And it's the cold in an old person's house that does the damage, when the electricity becomes too expensive and the damp creeps up. It rises from the ground and seeps in through the ridge tiles and runs through hidden webbed crevices in the walls until the entire house is musty and smells of old age. Glenasmole had been falling apart for two decades, even when you still slept upstairs, working your way up and down the steps on your backside, and the unused rooms were slipping into decline. That's when I put a commode in the corner of the dining room, beside the china cabinet, because there was no downstairs toilet. For years, you had refused to have one built. Someone even suggested an escalator that might be attached to the stairs – a small chair that would run on railings along the wall from hall to upper landing – but you said you heard of a woman who got on one of those contraptions and broke her hip trying to get off. So you weren't having any of that.

It was ever so; you had your own peculiar way of doing everything. You slept in a different room from your husband. You said he was a selfish man sometimes. And sometimes you flew into tempers when you were washing the dishes. You didn't like all his friends. And you said he didn't appreciate the way you slaved in the kitchen, cleaning and cooking and making ends meet on the meagre cheque he handed you at lunchtime every Friday when you were going into town on a bicycle to do the messages. And you never hugged him. In fact, you avoided touching for so long that eventually you divided the geography of the house between the both of you, each claiming separate spaces: the big bedroom his, the small bedroom yours, the front room his, and the kitchen all yours.

Of course, the nursing home was different. You found

246

other people again. Sometimes I'd go in and you'd say, 'Hello, Oliver,' confusing me with your brother because all of a sudden there were lots of people around and you became tender for one final moment as you were held by all of them; the living and the dead drawing you on to a new level of being in the world, where you let go of all your possessions, except for the handbag, a gaudy red plastic pouch that sat on the floor beside your chair in the day room for two years.

In the end you didn't even come to the day room any more. You lay in bed, and after another few months, you moved away from us completely in sleep, struggling with each breath on your final journey into silence.

But it was on the day of your departure from Farnham Road, heading for the nursing home, that my heart finally broke. I found it unbearable to sit downstairs in the kitchen, listening to you up there in the bedroom, going through your things, trying to decide what to take. And by accident you discovered some of those old photographs and mementos of long-ago weddings and you cried like a child. I felt ashamed that I was taking you away from your home – because it was your home. In the end, you brought nothing of any importance. Not even the photographs. It was as if you didn't want to remember anything at all after that, as you were driven away from the wrought-iron gates of Glenasmole for the very last time.

And there was so much I never said in that house and so

much you never told me; so many stories that were hidden, so much resentment that I stored up as I watched you for years putting food into your mouth in slow motion. So much of you in the air and in every room, until death finally claimed you and I could open all the windows and doors, and allow the house to breathe once again.

THERE IS MORE to life than just holding hands, and the English dictionary offers a variety of similar verbs – to hold on, to hold up, to hold out and to hold forth. There is a way of being held, and of beholding, which is not just touching or being physical but a way of holding each other that makes us human. In Tibet, the condition of being held is considered to be the ultimate reality of all things. The ultimate truth for Tibetans is not a god or a ground of being, but a dynamic whereby the entire universe is held, and holds itself, and holds us.

Holding each other. Holding everything. It's the ultimate reality. Everything else is a delusion.

And it's such a contentment to hold another human being, to abandon self-obsession, leave personal anxieties forgotten in the past, and reach forward towards other beings. It's the kind of bliss that everyone talks about when they talk about being in love. What the saints talked about when they talked about a union with God, an awareness that, despite the atrocities of life, you are always being held by someone.

It's like listening to Chopin. It's like being a child. I see it sometimes on a bus or train when a mother is holding a child. The two individuals melt into each other, and the mother becomes so fluid in her caress that it no longer matters whose body is whose. The mother says all and everything the infant needs to hear. And I think it's the same with lovers who have reached a certain stage in their lives. Maybe young love is not quite like this because, in the early years, love is passionate and unconscious and clings fiercely, but the assurance that you are held is something that grows stronger through the years. It's all in the wonder of letting go and trusting to another. It's the parachute jump without the parachute. It's even a bit like faith in God, as we understood it in the old days, the sense of letting go completely and trusting that the other person will hold you.

I used to have a poster on the wall of my student bedroom

many years ago. It was of an elephant clinging to a single daisy on the edge of a cliff. 'Hold me,' the elephant cried out. 'I will,' a voice replied from the clouds. 'Just let go.'

It was a nice, cosy little poster that didn't ring true to me at the time since history was full of people who hung over cliffs and let go and then fell into hell. And yet that image remained with me.

'Live your life with risks,' my old friend the General would say. 'Don't just walk over the cliff. Go over blindfolded and with the confidence that you can fly.'

You will be held.

When I first met the beloved I sang, 'Hold me close, and never let me go.' It was a song we hummed together in far-off countries, walking down unknown streets where other couples were leaning on balconies under blue skies. And when I was away from her, in distant cities, I always ended up on a balcony on Sunday morning, looking out at the other apartment blocks around me and thinking to myself that the world was full of people holding each other. I would drink mint tea with lemon juice, and imagine them feeling happy and safe and sleepy, all in their private little apartments around me, and I too would long for my beloved to hold me again.

Sometimes I say it when we are lying in bed. Sometimes when we are standing on the edge of the earth in Donegal where the waves fall onto the sand. Hold me. And I used to think it was risky. *She might reject me*, I thought. One of these days she might say, 'No, I won't hold you any more. I'm fed up holding you like you were some helpless imbecile.' And then where would I be?

I have said it on warm afternoons in July. And in the kitchen after midnight on Christmas Eve, when everyone had gone to bed. Hold me. It's like a prayer.

And we have held each other all over the place – on balconies, in trains and somewhere on the north side of Mumbai. I said it to her once on the roof of one of the Twin Towers, and on the back of a lorry as we were driven with other tourists through the Grand Canyon in Arizona. No matter how much I have been overwhelmed by exciting holidays, history, archaeology, or the size of the universe, or the amount of tequila left in the bottle, I could always rely on her. I could always say, 'Hold me.'

When we were first married, we bought an enormous bed in Boyle that took up the entire bedroom of our small cottage in the hills, and though we could do very little else in that space, at least we were able to lie quietly on Sunday mornings holding each other for the entire length of *Sunday Miscellany*.

I would lie there imagining people all over the world doing the same thing. Holding each other; in cities and remote villages, in apartment blocks, small cottages and under canvas roofs, or under straw roofs, or under no roof at all.

And you don't actually have to say the words. Sometimes

it's just a gesture. A woman on a Ryanair flight nudging closer to her husband, a man looking across the Formica table of a cheap restaurant at his partner as he seeks her approval before tucking into a large steak, or a young girl dropping her head onto her boyfriend's shoulder on the bus to Cavan. They're all saying the same thing in their own way; they're all reaching out to hold each other.

Some years ago, there was a homeless couple who died in each other's arms as they slept in a doorway off Capel Street in Dublin. They were frozen to death in a cardboard box one frosty night. They hugged each other until the state pathologist parted them. Their intimacy was frozen stiff on an ice-covered street. The milkman found them the next day in the doorway, their bodies entwined by a mix of hunger, pain and love. They were old, alcoholic and homeless, and their minds too were probably twisted with psychic wounds and trans-generational traumas that never saw the light of day. But they held. They held each other tenderly as they fell into the silence of the night.

And sometimes I think about young people in their intimate moments after orgasm. I imagine soft, sleepy males on the flat of their backs, like beasts of prey when there is nothing more to achieve, and I imagine their mates beside them in silence as they hold each other.

Their embrace is the sanctuary of the modern world. Just like the monks of ancient days who found the presence of their god in the breaking of bread, so people now find it

253

in that exquisite aftertaste of love-making, when they hold each other quietly. I suppose that's what the ancient monks meant about Christ being 'behind, before, above and in everything we do'.

It's what mothers do. It's what lovers do. It's what God used to do before we trusted each other. And it's what my beloved used to do before she went away.

THERE WERE TIMES after my mother died when I tried to evaluate what kind of a son she had reared – or what kind of a man had I become in the shadow of her long life. I thought about her every day. As I toured the country with a one-man show, she would sometimes appear unexpectedly, here or there, a ghost on a random street or behind a rack of clothes in some shopping arcade. At a checkout, I would notice an old woman counting her change, and I'd look at the back of her head and for a moment it was as if my mother was standing there.

I remember being in a car repair shop in Limerick six months later, looking for seat covers because there was a rip on the seat of the jeep. The man behind the counter had a beard, and a mug of tea, and he found me a pair of cheap covers and threw in a Padre Pio air freshener to sweeten the deal. I liked him. I enjoyed being with him. I wanted the encounter to continue. The sheer masculinity of tyres and chains and oils in canisters and a cement floor well-blackened from spilled motor oil attracted me. I suppose I am still unsure of myself in a man's world.

Maybe that's because I never really let my mother go. I kept her all about me until the day she died. I needed her to approve of me and to hold me as a child likes to be held.

She was so strong that I couldn't walk away from her. I didn't pack my suitcase and emigrate. I didn't harden myself by living out some great adventure in a foreign land or by turning into a brute in the fields with a spade. I stayed close to her. I paid her homage. I feared her. And where and when it was possible, I smuggled myself into an intimate collusion with other women, seeking not to seduce them but simply in every endeavour to be their accomplice.

So I really envied alpha males their certitude, their compulsive attachment to the hunt and the way they take themselves so seriously. But I can't say I've ever enjoyed chatting with them. Not that the man in the repair shop was an alpha male. He was funny and self-deprecating, and it occurred to me that there is a huge variety of men in the world. They're not all warriors. Outside on the streets, a man was collecting for a 'Men's Shed'. I gave him €1, stuck the 'Limerick Men's Shed' sticker on my lapel and then went off to a pub where I discovered yet another emanation of the masculine universe: a drowsy world of leather and wood, with whiskey glasses on the tables, and pints of Bulmers and Guinness on the counter. It was 11.20 a.m. Sky News was on mute. One man sat at the bar staring at the screen. Another man read the newspaper on the counter like it was his job. Most people were wearing cheap, unwashed fleece jumpers, old anoraks and denim jeans. I ordered a mug of tea and nursed it in a shaft of sunlight. Everyone watched the mute screen as if they could extract some meaning from images of plutonium processing in Tehran.

By coincidence, I met an Iranian man on the street within the hour, though I never mentioned plutonium. He was beautiful. His gestures were gentle and he spoke like a poet about the land he loved. He was standing outside a shop that sold Persian handcrafts. Beautiful patterns in various colours printed on cotton. I was looking for a bit of Velcro to patch the hole in the seat of the jeep because as it turned out the seat covers I had bought earlier didn't fit. He showed me his stock of handbags and rugs and wall drapes all printed with intense colours.

'These colours are beautiful,' I said.

'Yes,' he agreed, 'but the colours are from nature. Red comes from pomegranate and green from the skin of the pistachio nut and blue from the indigo flower and brown from the walnut.'

'Where are you from?' I wondered.

'Iran,' he said.

Then he showed me the wooden print blocks that are used in the process.

'It's an ancient craft in my country,' he said. 'And my country is like a mother to me.'

'It's beautiful work,' I agreed. His face was radiant.

'I guess there is more to Iran than the images on Sky News,' I said, and he smiled.

I thanked him for the Velcro and went off thinking that if I had been born a woman I could easily have fallen in love with such a man. Not that I would want to be a woman in that neck of the woods. I feel sad sometimes when I see women in black veils with just a slit for their eyes, as they wait obediently beside men in elegant suits at airport gates. And I wonder if a woman's veil is a comfort to a man, or is it because men are afraid of naked emotion that they seek to cover women. And it's not just in Arabia or Persia that men fear emotion. An Irish woman once told me that on her way into the hospital to view the remains of her recently deceased father, her husband turned to her and said, 'Your sisters will be in here so for God's sake don't start crying.'

And sometimes I don't want to be a man in any neck of the woods. Because I've often seen men brood but I've

258

rarely seen them weep. Sometimes, I walk with the General and he sits on some bench by a lake, and he looks at the water so that viewed from the side he might be a cast of Winston Churchill, a bulldog crouching, and I can hear him breathe when we're alone in the same room, but I can never discern his heart.

My mother had a great ability to display emotion, even to the point of tears. Her song was one of disappointment. When I was a child, she would sometimes display me to the public and startle the audience with phrases like, 'I would have loved a little girl.' No doubt had she lived in Arabia, they would have clothed her in an extra-large veil, to protect themselves from her immense emotions.

Even when I was a teenager, she could speak simple sentences – things like, 'Your father was never interested in dancing' – with enormous pathos, and tears would well up in her eyes as she sat in the front room with a nun who came occasionally from some parish outreach programme to enquire about her health. The two women would sit there watching the television and emitting large sighs of horror or compassion, depending on what the news was about. And I sat with them, veiled in an iron mask of indifference; the hard shell that I hoped would someday make me into a real man.

259

I T WAS THE beloved who transformed Mother's house. She began in February and I was amazed. In the end, it seemed so simple and such fun. She arrived with a Brazilian boy who appeared out of the blue and helped her with the painting. I went to Cavan one day to see the work and when I saw him, so young and brown as a chestnut without a shirt or vest, his skin leaping with light against the backdrop of white walls, I was speechless. The walls were as cold as a tomb and he stood there like some perfect brown angel smiling at me. The bed was gone from the dining room. There were ladders and wooden boards and paint tins everywhere. They'd been working for about a week by then.

First they had stripped back the wallpaper and painted all the rooms white. Then they pulled out all the carpets and filled four skips with old furniture. Beneath the carpet in the kitchen and in the hall they discovered the original red and cream tiles that had been laid down when the house was built. She had knelt down on them with a knife and scraped them clean with the meticulous attention of a Tibetan Lama, and it was her who got a builder to take the doors off and put new fresh pine doors on all the rooms.

One day, she saw a blue nightdress under the bed.

'What's this?' she wondered.

'Oh, that's just one of her old things I meant to get rid of,' I said, and I threw it into a black plastic bag destined for the skip.

So much went into that skip. The broken chairs, the old sheets, the useless bed, the faded curtains, the delph angels, the Child of Prague, the wardrobes, dressing tables and the music cabinet for holding old records.

The skip swallowed her life, her privacy, her illness and her death. It even swallowed the vinyl recordings of Beethoven's piano sonatas and the crackling voice of John McCormack which I used to hear rising through the floorboards of my childhood bedroom as I lay awake at night worrying about school homework.

261

One day the Brazilian boy found a box of hats; seven in all, including a feathery green cap, a white straw hat, a beret, and an extravagantly wide-brimmed blue hat like something a young woman might wear at the races. But the box was in tatters, and the Brazilian boy wanted to throw it out. When he asked me, I said I wanted to keep the hats.

There was also an empty suitcase beside the hatbox which had my father's initials on it. So the Brazilian boy decided to throw out the tattered hatbox and put my mother's head-gear into my father's suitcase, which seemed for an instant to bring them both together once again as he handed me the suitcase.

I took it home and it is now in the attic of our cottage in Leitrim, and I suppose in the distant future someone will be surprised by the comedy of a man's suitcase full of ladies' hats as they forage through all the tracks and traces of private anxiety and trivial obsessions that I in my time may leave in my wake.

By July 2013, the work was done. The rooms were painted with a second and final coat. Over the white base, they painted soft mushroom and burgundy red. And the chimneys were cleaned and the fires were lit.

We thanked the beautiful boy from Brazil for all his help, paid him handsomely before he vanished into the air again, and then we sat down in the front room on two new sofas; one for her and one for me. We drank a bottle of wine that we had bought in a supermarket in town, before going upstairs. Our matrimonial bed, which we had cherished for twenty years since we first bought it in Boles of Boyle, was now there in the back room, all covered with fresh linen and soft pillows. It was our first night to sleep over. And then, in the middle of the night, I woke because she was awake.

'What are you thinking of?' I wondered, but she didn't say.

The following morning was Grave Sunday, a day when the town gathers in the local cemetery to remember the dead who are buried there and to bless all the graves. We drove out for 3 p.m. The crowd had gathered and the priest was already walking around the graveyard in the blazing heat, casting holy water on the graves and on the heads of the faithful. The graves were so tightly laid together that it was almost impossible to find a standing place near my mother's plot, so I stood close to the church as my beloved pushed forward with a wreath for the tombstone.

An old man was standing near a tree. He saw me coming and pulled my elbow. Only then did I recognise him as Mr Dolan, the man with straw hair who had spoken to me at her funeral. He looked even more frail now. I stood with him, shoulder to shoulder, as he smoked a cigarette.

'Where are you living?' he enquired.

'Leitrim,' I replied.

He said, 'There's no good broadband in Leitrim. You'd be better in Cavan.'

263

'How do you know?' I wondered.

'About the broadband? Me daughter told me.'

'I think she's wrong,' I said, 'but I might do that anyway.'

'Do what?'

'Come and live in Cavan. Now that the mother's house is empty.'

The voice of the priest through the microphone was uneven in the wind, a humourless roar, like the sound of a machine crushing metal in a breaker's yard far away.

The old man said, 'There was a Leitrim clergyman one time, who became a bishop here in Cavan. And when he got the job, the Leitrim people bought him an Audi, so that he could swank around like the other prelates. But the new bishop registered the vehicle in Cavan because he didn't want to be seen driving through the lush lawns of his adopted county with Leitrim registration plates. Doesn't that say it all?'

I said, 'That surely says it all.'

From the high ground, we could survey the congregation, some with hankies on their bald heads, some with elaborate straw hats, and some with their deck chairs right on top of the grass beneath which their ancestors slept, as they all sheltered from the sun. The priest was perspiring in his heavy vestments.

'You're safe enough in Cavan,' the old man said.

I was wondering if he ever washed his enormous mop of straw hair or if he ever changed his clothes. I imagined him

264

in the same suit for decades, scything the fields in the heat of June and licking the frost off choc-ices in August, with perspiration dripping down his cheeks. Or did he ever wear the suit in bed, on winter nights, to keep his bones from freezing?

A family of rusty-brown cattle with yellow ear tags, dozed in a field beyond the graveyard.

Mr Dolan said, 'The problem with Cavan is the drumlins. The horizon is always a few feet away. You go round in circles to get to where you started from. Do ye know what I mean?'

The priest finished his prayers. Mr Dolan blessed himself.

'My mother's grave is over there beside the wall,' he said. 'She was buried in 1947; a white-haired woman in black shawls, with a chin that would split hailstones. And she could put the turf into the flames with her bare hands. But she was old when I got to know her, she'd spend her days remembering the dead – the lovely young boys who'd died on the roads, and in the Great War, and the old dotes who never woke up for their porridge, and those who were dead in drains or squashed by the plough or mangled by an unruly mare or cut in two in the trenches around the Somme.'

Then he looked over at my mother's grave and he said, 'She isn't here either.'

'Pardon?'

'You didn't get the tombstone done yet,' he whispered,

changing the subject. 'You'd need that done. Otherwise people would be wondering. You know what I mean?'

'I do,' I said. 'I'll be looking after it soon.'

'But she's not here,' he repeated, eyeballing me through the cloud from his smoking cigarette. 'She's in another place now. They're all gone home.'

And despite the blue sky at the top of the graveyard, we were engulfed in shadows from the trees behind us. The priest was finished. The people were scattering and we descended the hill as silent men trying not to disturb the dead. Having examined the world as poets do, and having prayed for the dead as Christians do, we went away with a great surge of vitality.

'Who was that fellow you were talking to?' my wife asked when I got as far as the jeep.

'I think his name is Gabriel,' I said. 'He's a Cavan man. Although I only know him as Mr Dolan.'

266 I never saw him again, because he too passed away in the autumn of 2013 and now rests in his own plot beside his mother, where the soil is still heaped up in a mound, near the wall beside the trees.

WHEN SHE WAS one year in the grave, I went back on the road doing readings and performances to earn a living. I toured between August and December 2013; cold, wet days and dark nights on the road, performing in arts centres and sleeping in the deluxe rooms of various hotels. It was a great adventure. I watched the universe unfold every night in a different lounge bar or in a different late-night takeaway.

One night, I met a man with a heart of stone. He was in a bar in a midland town and he leaned on the counter as he sipped his drink, nursing grudges. I listened to him for a while as he spoke of his mother and how she had hurt him. When he was finished his litany of neglect I said, 'That's awful.'

'No' he said, 'it's all in the past. I'm happy now.'

He clenched his fist around his glass of whiskey and he looked into it as if he was gazing at a knife that some day he might plunge into an unseen enemy.

'Yeah,' he repeated with a grimace, 'I'm happy now.' Though there was nothing in him that I could envy.

I confessed to him that I'm rarely happy.

The dogs in Leitrim are happy. They're well-minded. They yap cheerfully when the farmers head up the hills with fodder for cattle. The horses are happy, apart from those who live in fields of rushes, shivering in the freezing fog. But mostly it's true to say that animals, if well-minded, are reasonably happy. They fit into the natural universe in a way that I don't. I sit uncomfortably in the world, aware of myself, uneasy that the universe remains silent and refuses to reveal its secrets to me.

One wintry night in early December, with heavy rain and cold winds lashing the jeep, I checked into the Plaza Hotel in Tallaght. I was hungry.

A young man in the bar told me that his mother worked in a Chinese restaurant nearby and he recommended the Mongolian beef. 'It's her speciality,' he said. So we phoned her, and he spoke to her in a strange language and shortly afterwards the food arrived and I ate it in the half-light of the bar with a pint of cider to wash it down. It was delicious, and we passed an hour speaking about Mongolia, seaweed and the benefits of rice noodles.

On another occasion, I was in the Joinery in Smithfield to give a talk about Mongolia and orgasms and horses' milk. The Joinery is a small arts centre that offers creative resources to young artists. Afterwards, I chatted to a psychiatrist. She was drinking mulled wine and she had a lilting Ulster accent. I would have been happy to converse with her all night but I needed to push on. I had a gig in Cork two nights later.

I drove as far as Portlaoise that night, thinking about psychiatry and mental health and wondering if chemicals had the capacity to inject happiness into the human skull. I checked into a hotel where a few teenage girls wearing silver tiaras and pink ballerina costumes hung around an empty dance floor in the lounge. A DJ played music so loud that it was impossible to talk, and a few unruly boys sat at tables slobbering their drink and shouting into each other's ears. On a distant TV screen, Jeremy Paxman was talking to Russell Brand. I felt alone, but at least I wasn't pretending I was happy any more. I guess that food, sex and belonging in a tent are only moments on the road of life. And so too is grief. Maybe meaning is further down the track. 'It will come later,' I told myself. And in the meantime all I could do was keep travelling.

After the gig in Cork, I went to my hotel and ordered a drink and brought it to the residents' lounge. I was sitting on a big sofa when a woman came over to me.

'I hope you don't mind me sitting here,' she said, as she sat beside me and gazed across the lounge, avoiding eye contact.

'I read something that you wrote in the newspaper about your mother being a widow,' she said. 'Actually I'm a widow too,' she added, as if she was confessing something ugly. 'I'm fine most of the time, but I dread Christmas.'

'What was your husband's name?' I wondered.

She spoke it, and I felt his presence well up inside her as she began to weep. And then we shared so much detail about her life in twenty minutes that I couldn't stop thinking of her all through my trip.

'It was like an amputation,' she said.

And I just couldn't get her out of my mind, even during Christmas, so I tried writing to her for the New Year, the kind of letter that I would never have been able to write to my own mother when her husband had died:

> I was thinking of you over the Christmas and of the years that stretch before you now as a widow. And I was thinking of all the years you spent with your beloved and all the drama at the end of his life. And how familiar you were with his body and with all its curves and edges and the smell of the sheets. And now all you have left is the emptiness in the bedroom

270

when you walk into it, going from room to room, as if walking from one empty shell to another.

Believe me when I say that the house where my mother had lived became a shell too, where she tried to protect herself from loneliness after her husband died. But please don't protect yourself like that. Embrace the memories that you shared with me. The way he left things in the bathroom when he had finished washing, the sight of his clothes on the floor, the texture of his damp discarded towel. Don't hide from the terror of that absence. Don't be afraid to wonder how it might have been if you had grown old together. And when the grief has fully surfaced, make a mug of tea in the kitchen. Don't be afraid of that ritual you always did with him, that collaboration of boiling a kettle, or laughing through the soap operas.

And go for a walk in the garden. Examine the dead plants and the frosty clay that was so full of flower last July. Consider the resilience of cherry trees, the tight lawn's endurance and the understated dignity of sharp hedge lines that he trimmed for decades.

Walk along the avenue where in funereal solemnity he made his final journey away from you, out the gate on his sons' shoulders before they put his coffin in the hearse. You always worried about him leaving you, but you never thought he'd leave like that.

Walk back up the avenue and plan your future.

271

The flowerbeds will still need attention in January. Promise yourself to begin again. He is gone now. Last year will be on his gravestone and this is another year. Commit to it and to now – even if now is empty. And when the flowers are stale on his grave, bring new ones. Say they are for him, and leave them there and then walk away. Which is only what any of us try to do after a funeral, with the help of others.

AS I GET older I come closer to the type of isolation in which my mother had lived for years. And alone in Leitrim, two years after her death, I began to realise that life is almost comical in its brevity and in the hubris with which we live the early part of it. Nothing seems to be permanent, though I suppose that stories and the telling of stories is what matters.

And my story is that more than sex or death or the remote possibility of God, there was one thing more fundamental to my way of being in the world than any other, and that was the all-pervading influence of a mother; and not just her influence, but her presence and her love.

So I had a need to satisfy her. My desolation at not being successful was often catastrophic and sometimes drove me to alcohol and at other times to religion. And I suppose that going through the things in her house was a necessary way of clearing her presence completely from the earth.

I even made a pilgrimage to the Black Madonna of Częstochowa, in the monastery of Jasna Góra in Poland, a few weeks after she died. I suppose it was a way of acknowledging that my mother and the beautiful woman in Catholic iconography were intertwined, and I wanted to make my peace with both of them and I hoped that the psychic power of the Madonna would melt something in me – something hard and cynical that had grown inside me over the years.

Despite the enormity of Karol Wojtyla's achievements in history, his papacy always uneased me. His elevation to the Throne of St Peter marked the end of the Church that I had joined. The short spring of hope and Christian renewal which had begun during the Second Vatican Council was over as he and Joseph Ratzinger began grinding liberal theologians and philosophers into the ground, and creating a façade of sanctity and orthodoxy behind which so many children suffered abuse, so much abuse was hidden and so many people were left bereft of any shelter in the confusion and storms of their ordinary lives.

Maybe that's what happened to me. I couldn't belong in Joseph Ratzinger's Church, so maybe I cut myself off from the spiritual consolation of believing that there is someone beyond the stars that cares for us all with love. But there's a strange tenderness creeps up on me when I am emptied of dogmas about the substantial nature of the universe. The freedom from certainty makes me feel vulnerable, and I get a sense of what my teacher means when he says that this emptiness is the mother of compassion.

Usually when I've been to Poland over the years, I have tended to ignore the triumphal crosses on the streets of Warsaw or on the spires of medieval churches in Kraków. I was never quite in the humour of making pilgrimages to the Black Madonna at Częstochowa.

I was more interested in the story of those who had clung to the cliff for centuries, and who when they let go merely fell into the abyss at Auschwitz. I am not a Jew but sometimes in Polish ghettos I have had an overwhelming feeling of loss and absence and it's hard to believe in little elephants that hang from daisies or in any other sentimental religious posters that might suggest we could be saved by God if we would just let go.

I remember being in Łódź one winter, walking around the old Jewish ghetto in the snow, when I saw the full moon rise on a Friday evening. A pallid moon, it rose above the blackened trees and I felt so empty that I fled instantly back to the comfort of my hotel and had a hot bath.

The Grand Hotel on Piotrkowska Street is a world of old carpets, art deco, high ceilings and a hush of musty grandeur that has remained unchanged throughout the twentieth century; a hotel that has kept the hot water running and the doors opened continuously since then, and though I didn't notice any other guests in the dining room, the waiter spoke in whispers.

When I was passing a red-bricked church near where the ghetto used to be, I felt a lump of shame in my chest and found it difficult not to think harshly about the Roman Church and all the popes who followed so eagerly in the footsteps of the Roman Emperor Constantine, who first made an issue of the cross. In his visions the cross first appeared like an upturned sword, by which he might conquer the world and which caused him to go looking for the true cross – the thing that popes for centuries afterwards asserted the Jews had used to kill God.

276

I didn't feel much Christian fervour as the plane landed in Warsaw, nor on the train as it ploughed through the windy clouds of snow towards Łódź on the eve of the Sabbath, nor did I feel much confidence in any god as I walked the derelict streets that were once a ghetto to 700,000 Jews.

After the bath, I watched from my window as men on a cherry picker cleared ice from the roof. Then I downloaded images of the moon and the sour, dark alleyways and backstreets that I had taken with my phone – images of

young boys with ear-rings selling onions from the back
of a white van, an old man pulling two bags of coal on a
buggy as his wife lit a cigarette and held it to his lips in the
freezing fog, and a hatless woman who dropped her bag of
McDonald's food in the snow. I could smell the chips as
she sighed and I wanted to hug her and say, 'I know how it
feels to lose something.' But neither she nor I knew what it
might be like to lose everything.

And neither of us were Jews. At least it's not likely that
she happened to be one of that tiny remnant who survived
the Shoah.

The following day, I went to a Jewish restaurant and
devoured a bowl of chicken soup, as good as ever my own
mother made, but when I asked the girl who served me if
it was owned by a Jewish family, she smiled and said she
didn't think so.

I left for Warsaw that Sunday. A man on the railway
tracks in a yellow jacket was chatting on his mobile. I
suppose he was talking to his wife about what to get in
Tesco on his way home or some other ordinary business.

Snow always amazes me; the heaps of it stacked up and
the salty falling of it, and the cloudy fog of it, and the very
stillness in the middle of it.

But in a Polish monastery, I hoped I would find a way
to return to my faith. After all, I had been ordained a
Catholic priest, and though I resigned very shortly after
I was ordained, I had never been laicised. I had clung

quietly to the hope that all my devotion to the icons of my childhood would some day awaken in me once more what is called the grace of God. But I was nervous of going to such a conservative place as Jasna Góra. I suspected it might be dark and poor and full of rain and old women in damp coats and hats like they used to wear in Ireland in the 1960s. But it just seemed like the right place to go after my mother died.

So I travelled to Częstochowa in September. It was a bright autumn afternoon. The sky was blue. The town was asleep. The trees on the sidewalk were yellow. The supermarkets were open, but there wasn't much business. I bought a bottle of water and an apple. Derelict men hung about outside, smoking, lying on the ground, scratching their beards, and sizing me up as beggars do when they're about to beg.

A wide-open avenue inclined upwards towards the monastery, with trees lined on both sides. Young lovers smoked at street tables outside restaurants. There were men on bicycles and young girls walking dogs and couples just wandering with shopping bags or eating dainty fresh eclairs with their fingers as they strolled along. A pregnant woman in her twenties was waiting for me at the hotel reception, and she led me to a room with dark wooden floors and a black rug at the foot of a king-sized bed and a balcony looking out on the street. Tiny spotlights in the ceiling lit the room with a soft peach light and a jacuzzi in the

278

bathroom was lit by a red lamp on the wall. This was a very modern hotel and I thanked the pregnant woman and said I was delighted.

The monastery was different. It was surrounded by massive walls just beyond the leafy park across the road. I entered under the arch and along a cobbled avenue to the main church. The little cobbled street was silent like a medieval village, without traffic, apart from a few Franciscans in robes, nuns, priests, and old women coming and going from the church.

Some priests walked about with a great sense of humility, their heads bowed and their faces turned inwards, but others swaggered in their cassocks, eyed me with suspicion and authority, and some old nuns stood like generals at the door of the visitors' centre, like the countrywomen of my childhood who could rule their houses as little tyrants.

But it wasn't them I had come to see. I had come to 279 worship the sacred mother; she who is enshrined in the icon above the tabernacle, and who would soon enfold me in her tenderness. I blessed myself at the water font and stepped inside.

In the shaded church, poor people were kneeling and standing and walking and lighting candles. There were young nuns with slim bodies kneeling very still in the pews with such physical discipline that I could feel grace oozing from their stillness. A fat priest was saying mass on a side altar. A little bull of a man with red ears, he ploughed through the liturgy like he was starving and needed to get at his porridge.

And for everyone in the church, and for me as well, there was just one single focus for our attention. It was behind the railings of a small chapel, in the far corner; the Black Madonna, the exquisite and ancient icon that holds a glance more haunting that the *Mona Lisa* and more embracing. A red sanctuary lamp hung before the image and a silver monstrance holding the Blessed Sacrament sat on the white altar cloths below it.

The icon drew me in to pray and worship and to remember with nostalgia the gestures of devotion I had learned as a child. I felt years of alienation from the Church beginning to dissolve.

There was something so intense about the presence of love in the small chapel that no irony or cynicism could be tolerated. This was home. And I too had a right to be here.

'I am here in a safe place with you,' I whispered.

I remained for a few hours, sometimes sitting beneath the icon in close proximity and sometimes walking away, down the back of the church to sit in a pew remote from the others.

Sometimes I felt that the bodies of nuns around me were vibrating with love, and I watched how they prostrated themselves on the floor as they came and went. One particularly beautiful face wrapped in her nun's starch habit turned and gazed directly at me and for an instant I had a wild urge to prostrate myself before her. But I desisted, although we did kneel a long time side by side before the icon. And the more I offered my body in reverence to this mother, the closer I felt to the men and women around me, as if in some very deep way we were brothers and sisters.

When the bells rang, a little priest came out as chirpy as a cuckoo from a clock and sang the mass in Latin. I went to the altar to receive the sacrament. And as the litany of the saints washed over me, a great sense of remorse overwhelmed me and I began to cry.

I don't understand what happened that day. It certainly didn't reawaken in me any fervour for religion. But it did heighten my awareness that without some connection with the great mother of all things, and without acknowledging her grace in the air, in the trees, the mountains, sea and sky, I would be lost forever.

While the beloved was in Poland, I turned to the east, reading sutras on my Kindle and watching the Dalai Lama and Thich Nhat Hanh on YouTube. In fact, I even improved at the meditation. I suppose everything is a question of practice. And through the six weeks of her absence I had gradually become accustomed to the silence. Each day passed without much event. The postman would throw more pamphlets from various political parties in the letterbox around noon. I collected my takeaway lunch in Drumshanbo around 1 p.m. and ate out of the small silver dish in the kitchen listening to the tail end of the RTÉ news. In the afternoons, I dozed at the stove, though gradually the weather improved and, by April, Leitrim was enjoying a foretaste of summer.

I spent a lot of time talking to birds, the horse in the field next door, the cat, Simone Weil and other folks whom I conjured out of the air. Even my dreams became clearer, and I dived into them at night like a swimmer in the water.

One night, I dreamed that the president of Russia was a cuckoo bird on my roof, and he was shaking the chimney, because our chimney is not in good condition and of course in winter the strong winds blow the rain up the tiles, underneath the flashing so that the white walls of the cottage turn brown along the line of the chimney breast. So the idea that the president of all the Russias was up there with claw feet shaking the chimney pot did me no good at all. And what was worse, he was wearing no clothes, and his skin was covered in feathers. Of course, this was only a dream. But I didn't know that, because we don't know we're dreaming when we're dreaming. I thought I was lying outside on the grass beneath the clear sky and that the cuckoo flew off the chimney and hovered above me, blocking the sun.

I woke up in distress, but at least I was in bed. It was about 7 a.m. and I could hear the real Mr Cuckoo singing his song farther up the mountain, near Scardan Waterfall, which is the spot where he seems to announce himself every year.

Later, I was in the studio, wondering if it was time to close up the stove for the summer, when a swallow flew in the glass patio door, carved a circle in the space above me, and landed on one of the rafters that crosses the apex roof.

'I used to live here,' he said.

I said, 'No, you never did, this was only built last year.'

'Well,' he said, 'there was a green shed on this exact spot when I came in previous summers. And now it's gone.'

'Yes,' I confessed, 'there was a green galvanised shed here but I was obliged to take it down in order to build this lovely studio.'

'Well,' he said, 'it's not so lovely for me, is it? Where am I supposed to go for the next five months to rear my little chickens?'

His feathers were oily black with a tint of blue.

'Can I stay here?' he seemed to ask, as he shifted sideways on the rafter.

'Absolutely not,' I said, 'because my beautiful wooden floor would be destroyed with bird poo. And I couldn't keep the door open all the time and besides, if you were coming and going you might bang your head off the glass and kill yourself.'

He was devastated. He looked around him once or twice, and then flew out the door without farewell. I sat on the step outside the door staring at the lake. Absorbing sounds from the garden. Absorbing colour and light and the movement of birds and the smell of the yellow gorse

283

that was starting to bloom. Great heaps of sensation flowed through me, and I didn't bother to analyse what they were or what was me.

I kept remembering that my mother was wearing a green cardigan and a pale cream frock in her coffin, with a silver broach pinned to the lapel of the cardigan. I could see her still, the face all powdered and polished with rouge and lipstick, as if that could protect her body from the worms. But yet, beneath the clothes, I could sense her nakedness in death. When we die we can hold no more. That is the exquisite sorrow of it.

And I remember too that just to sit sometimes with the beloved, and breathe in unison and know we were alive, even if we were only watching some banal programme on the television, seemed like an enormous miracle. Sometimes watching soap operas was like a lazy falling into semi-consciousness. The programmes were so vacuous and shallow that sitting passively before the moving images felt like entering into a void. And yet, in the void, we could feel time passing and in the passing of time we could feel our hearts cry out to each other in love: Hold me.

The old Asian proverb kept coming back to me. 'If you name the bird you cease to experience the song,' and I began to suspect that my mind had finally come home to my body, as Thich Naht Hanh says.

Later that morning, I made a decision. I loitered around the gates to the roadway, admiring the primroses beneath the branches of the wild rose and realising that spring had already arrived. I was waiting for the postman. When his white van drove up, I asked him if he could assist me in the small matter of removing a piece of furniture from the house.

He agreed and we went indoors and I showed him the fifty-inch television.

I said, 'I'd like to put this thing in the shed.'

'Jesus,' he declared, 'that's a beautiful television.'

As we lifted the huge screen, I could see his face crunch into a tight muscular squeeze and he went beetroot red. I was wondering what would happen if he had a heart attack. Might he be insured by An Post? Or might our house insurance cover it? You can never be too careful.

'Christ,' he said, 'this is heavy.'

It was, but eventually we got it out the door and around the back of the house into one of the dry sheds.

'That'll do,' he said.

'That'll do,' I repeated.

He handed me a brown envelope. It was the bill from the solicitor for all the work done on the property in Cavan.

'No love letters,' he joked.

'No love letters,' I repeated.

I didn't tell him that during the year I had read too many old love letters that I myself had written forty years earlier. I came upon them by accident one day in an upstairs wardrobe in Cavan. Letters that I had composed to girlfriends and never sent; some that they had sent to me. Letters that had been forgotten for decades.

And they weren't complimentary. For the most part, I was condemned in the scrawl of several young women as a cold fish and a man frightened of trusting other people.

But time passed. We all grew old. And I would hardly remember their names now except that my mother for some reason stored the letters in a suitcase, underneath a silver photo album that tracked her own honeymoon in 1950 from the Bush Hotel in Carrick-on-Shannon to Galway, the Cliffs of Moher and around the Ring of Kerry. Her album was stuffed with photographs, of herself, with a worried brow, or of him posing at the bonnet of his Ford car, and in one picture both of them hugged and smiled like children under Daniel O'Connell's monument in the middle of Ennis. Maybe she put my photos with her own by accident and then forgot about them. Or maybe she actually read my willowy love notes and saw some comic contrast between the formality of her own happy honeymoon and the litany of my sins and sorrows as enunciated by a variety of honest young women.

During those six weeks alone in Leitrim, I often sat on a garden seat beneath the huge Chilean beech trees, their long, extending branches of hard green leaves reaching across the lawn, and the silver birch and downy birch bending to the east from twenty years of windy winters, and the white flowering jasmine, and the spinosa wild rose that came from Sligo, and the chestnut that Paul and Anne had given us as a wedding present in 1993, and the oaks that were blessed by my teacher the Panchen Ötrul Rinpoche, and the yew that a monk from Tibet had planted, and all the other trees and living things that were beginning to show life and bud at the end of a cold March. The cottage had deteriorated. It was filthy. I had not hoovered it. I had not washed the dishes nor turned on the dishwasher. I had not made nor changed the bed in two weeks. But in the garden, I felt emotionally clean and spiritually naked. My self-obsession dissolved like the morning dew and I became aware of the world. My mind was clear.

So I sat with Simone Weil and beautiful swallows and the odd dark cuckoo, and sometimes near the willows I turned to gaze on Simone Weil but there was only me beneath the trees. I turned to find my mother too, or some other saint, but they were all gone. The garden was empty.

Lough Allen was blue. The sky was blue and cold. A long tuft of white cloud like cotton wool hung on the ridge of 287 Sliabh an Iarainn. Around me the alder trees and primroses were flourishing. The slope of the lawn was riddled with holes where the badgers fed at night. In the woods behind where I was sitting, there was a carpet of snowdrops. A single magpie stood guard high up in a Scots pine. And along the beech hedge, a wren was hopping about looking for things I knew nothing about.

I still remember a bronze relief I saw on the wall of a church as I was on my way to the monastery of

Częstochowa. I was in Warsaw waiting for the afternoon train and I decided to walk into Old Town and on New Street I saw a huge figure of Christ carrying his cross, outside the majestic doors of a church, and I went inside, which is where I found an image of Mary, holding not Jesus but a dying soldier. Her two hands were clasping his head to her breast. The mother's loving face was in the foreground, her big eyes as sad as if she were holding her son. And I had to pay attention to it. I knew it was a soldier because there was a hole in the back of his head. A hole as perfectly round as a pistol shot and there was no hope for him. But yet she held him. It could have been an image from Afghanistan or Syria or any airport terminal where a woman stands and waits for a bodybag. I remember being moved by the sad face of the woman. It wasn't as if I was looking at anything divine. The soldier was clearly human. And so was she. It was just a simple and undeniable affirmation of human compassion and for no particular reason it reminded me of an incident that happened when I was a child.

It happened in the afternoon when I had just come home from school. I took a young kitten out of the cardboard box in the kitchen where it had made its bed and the animal was instantly terrified. It ran everywhere to escape me. It jumped up on chairs, and then the table and onto the worktop. I realised that Mother had left a cooker ring on and it was red hot. I could feel the heat from the metal. The kitten was on the worktop. If I jumped at her, she might jump onto the ring. So I thought maybe it would be better to stand still. Don't frighten her further. But she actually walked determinedly towards the plate until her paw connected with the red iron and stuck to it, sizzling for a moment, and then she screamed and flew through the air and ended up behind the washing machine and the old Jacob's biscuit tins in the scullery that were used for holding wrenches. And she wouldn't come out.

I lay on my side telling her I was sorry. I hadn't meant to hurt her. Her eye watched me. She didn't know what had happened. She didn't know how she had been hurt, or who had done it – though she probably suspected me. In the darkness, I could see just her eye between the tins and the washing machine. But she kept looking at me. And I stayed there. I kept looking at her until, eventually, she came out and let me hold her. I held her for a long time, petting her, and both of us were terribly upset. After a while I knew she felt grateful to be comforted. I knew she liked being held. I knew that the pain had woken in her an intensity of awareness about the savagery of sentient life and in that pain she felt strangely better because she was being held.

After that, we were great friends. Her paw healed and she loved nothing better than to jump up on my lap when I came from school and be held by me. And I loved holding her. And my mother never blamed me for taking her out of the box. And I never blamed my mother for leaving the cooker on.

BY THE TIME the beloved arrived home from Poland, the season had changed. The winter was over. Spring was well developed and because of the warm weather it felt like summer. It's not as if she had been away for years. It was only six weeks. But I was up at 7 a.m. and I went mad fussing around the house, cleaning dishes and floors and worktops and emptying the cat's tray that had been unchanged for over two weeks.

She had travelled across Europe and trudged in the snow along foreign streets and met new friends and learned all sorts of new stuff about Fresco Art and Expressionist painting, and she would have new ideas now about the meaning of life, because that's what happens when you leave your comfort zone and go to another world for a few weeks. But I was at home with the elephant; the enormous conundrum of the human mind. And it settled. Just occasionally it settled, and was still and present to the rustling leaf and the buzz of life around me.

Every day, I had sat on the floor, with my back straight, in front of a small candle as the cat sat on the opposite armchair watching me with one eye, a paw covering the other eye and half her head.

At 8.30 a.m. on a beautiful spring morning, I finished my meditation and, without the slightest compassion, I threw the cat out. She wasn't impressed. 'The beloved is coming,' I explained. 'She might even now be in the air over Germany heading for Dublin airport. We mustn't be sleeping all day today.'

I imagined throwing my arms around her saying, 'So tell me everything.'

'Where do I begin?' she would reply. 'I have had so many adventures!'

That's the way it used to be in the old days in good hotels, when we had been separated for a while and were suddenly back together again. We would run the hot water and plant the condoms under the pillow and arrange the bed before getting into the bath. Those were afternoons

I loved. And afternoons were the best moments for love, or so I read in a poem by Ovid when I was a teenager. 'Afternoons were the best,' Ovid had said. And I stuck to that proposition and I found it to be true.

Before heading to Dublin to meet her I filled a tiny suitcase with some fresh clothes and a toilet bag. I put the laptop in my briefcase, with the flexes, adapter and a phone charger. And I took walking boots and my rain gear too, flung them all into the back of the jeep as if I was heading off trekking in the mountains.

Then I was nearly off. The engine was running. Except that I decided to go back and double-check the electricity and the central heating and make sure that the kettle was plugged out. And, of course, the cat had slipped back in a window. So I got her by the underbelly and left her outside again.

I reversed slowly out the gate. The cat had now hunched into a tight bundle of misery at the gable wall. It was almost 10 a.m. I drove down the slopes of Mount Allen, the lake on my left spread for eleven miles and the mountain behind it. I went through Drumshanbo and on towards Ballinamore. I was almost in Cavan when I got a text. I saw her name and pulled over to read it.

Apparently she was still in Warsaw. She was stuck in Warsaw. She had mistaken the month when she was booking her return flight. She had clicked 'April' when she ought to have clicked 'May' and when she got to the check-in at Modlin airport the lady said that there was nothing she could do to help. So she had to book another flight, and then another night in her hotel and then go back all the way on the bus to Warsaw with all her luggage. I don't think she would have been too happy about that but she was actually apologising to me and hoping that it didn't inconvenience my plans.

'No problem,' I texted back. In fact, I was delighted. I would have an extra evening in the city.

I arrived at the hotel in Ballsbridge around 3 p.m., checked in and immediately booked a ticket online for the Project Arts Centre later in the evening. I'm a creature of habit.

Driving back along the same canal, and checking into the same hotel and even going to a show in the same theatre as I had done on the day she had left were all a kind of ritual of repetition that made me feel secure.

The show was called *Visitation*. It was a collaborative work between a Butoh dancer, a musician and a sculptor. I took my seat in the racked auditorium of old-fashioned seats and I could see the Butoh dancer, standing on the edge of the stage, pallid and undefined among the shadows. When the show began, he moved slowly across the stage for an hour like a ghost or a moon; a human without a narrative, broken like a victim of war and silent like an imbecile.

It was an exquisite experience. It didn't offer any clear

293

narrative or storyline. Just a human being in motion, full of anxiety on the surface, and yet deep down in his movement, I felt a sense of longing, a connectedness with people in the audience, as if he was trying to assure us of his enduring love for us. I read it like a poem, a kind of love in a time of cholera. And I felt an intense connection with the dancer, as if we were a single being, feeling the same disturbance, and that he there on the stage was just expressing in his body what was buried in my heart.

I couldn't wait to tell the beloved about it the following day.

I returned to the hotel and enjoyed a couple of brandies in the bar, chatting to a young waiter from Bulgaria. I was excited. Then I went upstairs and opened a bottle of wine, which was meant for the beloved, except that she was stuck in Warsaw so now it was just myself and Vincent Browne again, and Vincent couldn't drink with me since he was on television and I could hardly push a glass through the screen.

I also had two brandy glasses, because I didn't want to be seen carrying a single brandy to the bedroom. So I pretended I had company, as I was ordering my two final drinks. That way if I met someone in the lift they wouldn't think I was a sad bastard drinking alone. And in a sense I wasn't alone, because the Butoh dancer was still with me. I imagined him following me after I left the theatre, naked and white and taunting me, like a messenger from beyond the cliff, to let go and awaken.

He was so close behind me and so vivid in my imagination that when I opened the door of the room, I turned around and spoke to him.

'Here,' I said, 'hold this,' meaning the tray on which my two brandies rested. But as I spoke, a woman coming out of a door across the corridor saw me talking to myself, which caused me in turn to let one of the glasses slide off the tray and break. The other one I managed to save with my other hand.

'Fuck it,' I hissed, which undoubtedly the woman heard as she strode down the corridor, her high heels making not the slightest sound on the deep pile of cream carpet, although she did turn at the lift and gazed back down the corridor at me and smiled.

'Now look what you made me do,' I hissed at the Butoh dancer, when I got inside the room. 'I lost a brandy over you.'

Outside I could hear ambulances in the traffic, rain hitting the windowpane and the wind stretching the branches of the trees inside the railings of the car park. *It's funny how I'm always spilling drink*, I thought.

And in fact when the beloved came through the glass doors of the customs area in Dublin airport the following afternoon, I was holding a paper cup full of coffee which I waved to signal – *I'm here* – and the coffee spilled over my head. She was pulling a case on wheels, with two smaller bags hanging around her neck. We fumbled a hug and she looked at the coffee dribbling down my cheek and smiled.

We got a taxi. The driver was from Cameroon. I asked him about racism. He said sometimes people flag him down, make him do a U-turn because they are so desperate for a taxi and when he pulls up and they realise he is black they wave him on or tell him to fuck off. 'It is not nice,' he said.

After that I whispered my questions.

'How was the trip?'

'What did you eat?'

'Had you many perogis?'

'Were you at the opera?'

In the hotel, the Bulgarian waiter smiled.

'How are you this afternoon?' he enquired.

'I am well,' I replied, and before I could say more he spoke again.

296

'Shall I get you your usual, sir?' Like I was James Bond.

So we took the drinks to the room, my Miss Moneypenny and I, and when we were inside the door she started rummaging in her cases, checking that everything was there, opening presents she had bought for various people and showing them to me and asking what I thought.

I filled the bath and she lay on the bed. She said the water was too hot so I got in first and soaked and then came out wearing a white bathrobe and a new pair of silk pyjamas I bought at the airport while I was waiting. She was looking up at the ceiling.

'So,' she said, stretching on the bed, 'any news?'

'I made soup,' I declared. 'Chicken soup.'

'Great.'

'I have a big pot of it. Sitting at home on the cooker. We can have it tomorrow.'

'And no other news?'

I looked in her eyes.

'No,' I said. 'No news at all.'

I suppose I could have mentioned the television, but already the past had swallowed up all that had happened over six weeks. And, besides, I was holding her in my arms once again.

Acknowledgements

THANKS ESPECIALLY TO my brother Brendan, and to all Nellie's family, relations, neighbours and friends in Cavan who supported her with love through the years. Special thanks to the home help, care workers, Health Service personnel and Active Age volunteers who sustained her when she lived at Glenasmole, and to the staff of Newbrook Nursing Home in Mullingar for their immeasurable kindness in her final journey. Thanks to my partner Cathy for her love and wisdom, and to Sophia for brightening up so many birthdays for her granny. Thanks also to Simon Carman, Philomena Brown, Kathleen and Ann McGrenra, and to so many more who constructed a fabric of love and kindness over the years around the person we all knew as 'Nellie'.

It was a privilege to work again with Ciara Doorley, editor at Hachette Ireland, whose insight and skill guided me in the writing of this book, and I thank her for her faith and encouragement. And thanks to my agent Jonathan Williams for his vigilance as always with the text, and to Jenny in Scollans who made all the dinners.